Waking to a Nightmare

Deceived by a Charming, Narcissist Paedophile

Aminia Mayo

Waking to a Nightmare
Deceived by a Charming, Narcissist Paedophile

Copyright © 2024 by Aminia Mayo

All rights reserved.

No part of this publication may be reproduced, distributed, or transmitted in any form or by any means, including photocopying, recording, or other electronic or mechanical methods, without the prior written permission of the publisher, except as permitted by U.S. copyright law. For permission requests, contact the author.

Waking to a Nightmare
Deceived by a Charming, Narcissist Paedophile

For privacy reasons, some names, locations, and dates may have been changed.

Waking to a Nightmare
Deceived by a Charming, Narcissist Paedophile

DEDICATION

I dedicate this book to all those who have suffered at the hands of a narcissist and/or a paedophile. I hope this book helps you reveal your story, and by doing so, your mind is freed of trauma so that you can enjoy a beautiful life, as I am now doing.

My thoughts are with you.

Waking to a Nightmare
Deceived by a Charming, Narcissist Paedophile

ACKNOWLEDGEMENTS

My parents have always been there to support me.

My close friends stood by me and helped me to recover.

Those who encouraged me to write this story.

Waking to a Nightmare
Deceived by a Charming, Narcissist Paedophile

CONTENTS

DEDICATION iv

ACKNOWLEDGEMENTS v

ABOUT THE AUTHOR viii

PREFACE ix

PROLOGUE x

PART 1 – THE FIRST GENERATION

CHAPTER 1 12

CHAPTER 2 20

CHAPTER 3 30

CHAPTER 4 42

CHAPTER 5 51

CHAPTER 6 59

CHAPTER 7 69

CHAPTER 8 79

CHAPTER 9 88

CHAPTER 10 94

Waking to a Nightmare
Deceived by a Charming, Narcissist Paedophile

CHAPTER 11 108

CHAPTER 12 117

CHAPTER 13 128

CHAPTER 14 137

CHAPTER 15 149

CHAPTER 16 156

CHAPTER 17 161

CHAPTER 18 167

CHAPTER 19 174

CHAPTER 20 178

CHAPTER 21 182

CHAPTER 22 187

PART 2 – THE NEXT GENERATION

CHAPTER 1 192

CHAPTER 2 197

CHAPTER 3 203

CHAPTER 4 209

FOOTNOTES 215

Waking to a Nightmare
Deceived by a Charming, Narcissist Paedophile

ABOUT THE AUTHOR

Aminia first came to Australia when she was a small child. She grew up in a leafy green valley in NSW, Australia, surrounded by a loving family and many friends.

After finishing school, Aminia took a gap year before accepting a position at University the following year. During that time, she wrote articles and short stories for the university paper and was praised by her English Professor for her efforts. Aminia also wrote stories and articles for various community papers. Aminia says, *'My greatest joy was encouraging children to express themselves through writing.'*

Four years ago, Aminia joined a writing group. The members helped her refine her skills, and her writing expanded.

Aminia says, *'Many of the philosophies I hold high in my life are expressed in my writing.'*

Aminia developed community newspapers and supported school children in contributing articles. Of course, she also submitted her own stories and articles.

Aminia is also a keen artist, has won prizes in art shows, and enjoys sculpting. Unfortunately, all her records were taken by her narcissist husband when they split up as is revealed in this book.

Waking to a Nightmare
Deceived by a Charming, Narcissist Paedophile

PREFACE

Growing up, my mother used to say, *'You make your bed; you lie in it.'*

This meant that whatever happened in your marriage, you stuck in there and saw it through. There was no other way. There was no respite. There was no escape. Your job was to make it work, no matter what the circumstances.

I ask readers not to judge me on today's attitude regarding paedophilia. When this story unfolded, there was very little support for the victims and their supporters. The authorities, supposed to support victims, fell well short of doing that. Times have changed more recently, thankfully. However, there is still a long way to go.

I lived with a NARCISSIST AND A PAEDOPHILE.

This is my story.

Waking to a Nightmare
Deceived by a Charming, Narcissist Paedophile

PROLOGUE

'Dad, get off me! Leave me alone! I was asleep!'

My eyes flew open. I glanced at the clock—1:57 a.m. My feet hit the floor.

Standing at my daughter's bedroom door, my blood ran cold. It was as if the whole world had ceased to exist… and only this moment was left, gnawing at my insides.

My husband, Ivan, was lying on top of my 14-year-old daughter.

Waking to a Nightmare
Deceived by a Charming, Narcissist Paedophile

PART 1 –

THE FIRST

GENERATION

Waking to a Nightmare
Deceived by a Charming, Narcissist Paedophile

CHAPTER 1

My father was born in South Africa and immigrated to Australia when he was eighteen. He loved his new country and was eager to adopt its culture, and he soon became a real Aussie. When he turned twenty, he met my mother, and he declared that it was love at first sight. Dad's love for my mother was shown in many ways: loving words, bunches of flowers, presents, beautiful cards, and potted plants. That was the relationship I desired to have. I never witnessed any arguments between my mother and father. However, I'm sure they must have had some.

In the realm of my adolescent years, the budding romances portrayed in movies and novels held a mesmerising allure. They painted a picture of perfect enchantment, where young men courted the bashful damsels with patience and unwavering devotion—like many others, I yearned for my

Waking to a Nightmare
Deceived by a Charming, Narcissist Paedophile

own Prince Charming, hoping that one day, fate would present him to me.

Then, fate cast its spell, delivering a charismatic figure into my world. His charm and magnetic presence were impossible to resist. From the moment we met, he swept me off my feet, igniting within me a whirlwind of emotions I had never experienced until that moment. Was this chance encounter holding a promise of a love story straight out of those romantic stories I loved reading? Little did I know that this encounter would shape my life in ways I could never have imagined.

It was my first day at university. After unpacking my belongings in my room, I decided to walk around the campus to stretch my legs after my uncomfortable, lengthy trip on a cramped train.

Soon, a piano and laughter drew me to a door. I peeked in. The room was crowded with male adolescents. Being a lone female in a group of young men was uncharted territory for

Waking to a Nightmare
Deceived by a Charming, Narcissist Paedophile

me, and indeed, my father, who still held some of his old ways, would have forbidden me to enter such a place without a chaperone.

I was about to bolt when one of the young men saw me. He smiled and beckoned for me to enter. I hesitated before stepping through the door. Inside, I looked for an empty seat. The only one I could find was next to the pianist. As his fingers danced across the keys, I felt a comfort I hadn't known for a while. I was homesick, being so far from my family and friends. His music took me back to those memorable times around my grandmother's piano. We, kids, would sing and dance around in the company of our parents.

As if hypnotised by a Pied-Piper, I listened to the music while I took hooded glances at the piano player. His head bowed over the keys, and his golden hair flopped over his forehead and bobbed to the music. His fingers executed one last flourish on the ivories. He turned to me. My heart missed

Waking to a Nightmare
Deceived by a Charming, Narcissist Paedophile

a beat as his blue eyes stared into my dark brown eyes, and his lopsided grin caused me to blush.

'Hi there, miss err, what shall I name thee?'

Had I been pulled into a Shakespearean play? It did feel so. 'Ah, my name…is A-Aminia. This is my first day here.'

This Romeo's beguiling smile melted me. 'Well, A-Aminia, I'm very pleased to meet you,' he said, lifting my hand from my lap and shaking it.' May I walk you to your dorm?' I felt overwhelmed, as though I was treading in deep water, but overriding all trepidation, I felt flattered.

I hesitated before replying, 'Um, no need; I am in Dorm 1, just up the road.'

He combed his long fingers through his hair and grinned, 'Well now, A-Aminia, I can't let a pretty little thing like you walk around on your own after dark, now, can I? What sort of a gentleman would I be then, eh? My name is Ivan.' This

Waking to a Nightmare
Deceived by a Charming, Narcissist Paedophile

charming man did an exaggerated bow, and a lock of his hair fell over his forehead.

He certainly was a handsome, disarming character. As we stepped from the Music Room, he slipped his hand around mine and interlaced our fingers…exhilarating emotions swirled through me. My feet stumbled as I stepped up the curb on the side of the road outside my dorm. Ivan steadied me with his strong arm, then positioned himself before me. I lowered my red face to hide my embarrassment. He gently lifted my head with a finger under my chin. As I looked into his eyes, shining from the light of an overhanging streetlamp, I felt a strange kind of electricity moving through my body. Was I making a connection with him? I didn't know.

Still reeling from the strange feelings coursing through me, I was startled when he turned my head and kissed my cheek, then whispered, 'Goodnight, Aminia. I hope we meet again tomorrow evening in the music room.'

Waking to a Nightmare
Deceived by a Charming, Narcissist Paedophile

I was a shy and unworldly eighteen-year-old, and at that moment, this golden-headed Romeo caused feelings to rise in me that I had not experienced until then. As my unsteady feet found their way to my room, my heart drummed against my chest. Had I stepped into a scene straight out of a romantic movie? My mind believed so.

The following night, I almost skipped to the music room. Not only did "Romeo's" piano playing make my pulse quicken…, but his intoxicating cologne delighted my senses, adding to the romantic atmosphere.

From then on, meeting with him became a regular thing. One of my professors joked, 'Have you noticed you are wearing a dip in the step where you stand to be high enough to kiss your Prince Charming?'

Later, I discovered my English Professor was not so taken with Ivan. 'Aminia, why would you go out with him? Ivan doesn't have a creative bone in his body. You, on the other hand, are one of my brightest students. Don't let him mess

Waking to a Nightmare
Deceived by a Charming, Narcissist Paedophile

your creative mind.' His disapproval added a layer of tension to our budding romance, but I was too smitten to take this seriously.

Soon, Ivan and I were inseparable. We enjoyed roaming the hills near the university grounds, and Ivan always carried an overcoat over his arm no matter the weather. I thought how gallant this young man was when he spread his coat for us to sit on. And, as our friendship grew, we would cosy up on it while we cuddled and kissed. Had I fallen into a fairytale?

But there was 'someone' else in my fairytale—my thorn in a most beautiful romantic landscape. Ivan had been going out with another student before I arrived, and one of his friends told me they were still strong together. My stomach tightened and churned, and I questioned his sincerity regarding our developing relationship…was he genuine or simply playing with me?

I mustered the courage and questioned Ivan about this other student. 'Aminia, don't worry. My friend is nothing more than that. You must know you are the only one for me. The girl you are worried about has not been well, and I only visit to help her.'

Relief coursed through my body before my stomach tightened from the guilt caused by doubting him. Later, I found out Ivan saw her after he had left the university, and again, he assured me it was only a friendship. Another of my mother's often-expressed sayings echoed in my mind, '**Jealousy is a curse.**' And so, I berated myself for my destructive thoughts and feelings, resolving to ignore my doubts and allow our relationship to blossom.

In every fibre of my body and soul, I wanted Ivan and me to have a solid and lasting relationship.

I LIVED IN A DREAM AS A NIGHTMARE LINGERED IN THE SHADOWS AROUND ME.

CHAPTER 2

I basked in the love and attention of a caring and affectionate man. Ivan caused exhilarating feelings within my body. As the end of my first year approached, everything seemed infused with excitement and promise. However, amidst the joy, a dreaded date was coming up fast… Ivan would graduate a year before I did, leaving me behind. His first appointment was hundreds of kilometres from me. My stomach clenched as my thoughts dwelled on this, and unshed tears stung my eyes. I berated myself, *Come on, Aminia, pull yourself together; you can see your Romeo every semester break.'*

However, the hand of fate had another direction for me. In the last few months of that year, my health took a turn for the worse. I suffered from extreme fluctuations in energy, swinging from highs of exhilaration to bouts of intense lethargy. Fainting episodes became frequent, causing this

Waking to a Nightmare
Deceived by a Charming, Narcissist Paedophile

shy teenager much embarrassment. I was unaware that a severe hormone imbalance was wreaking havoc within my body, worsening daily.

Navigating my final semester became arduous as I struggled to complete assignments, and panic set in. How could I possibly study for my exams amidst the relentless grip of frantic energy one moment and extreme exhaustion the next?

I visited a local doctor, but he could not diagnose my ailment. He prescribed an antibiotic that did nothing to alleviate my worsening condition. The university nurse offered me aspirin. I did not have a headache, so this gave me no relief. Despite the difficulty, I managed to push through and complete my assignments and exams. My only comfort was the unwavering support and distraction my relationship with Ivan provided me.

At the end of the year, my mother arrived to drive me home. When she saw how the deteriorating state of my health had affected my body, she was horrified. She hugged me tight

Waking to a Nightmare
Deceived by a Charming, Narcissist Paedophile

and exclaimed, 'Oh my darling, I didn't know how bad your condition was; you should have told me.'

Minutes after we arrived home, my mother secured an urgent appointment with our local doctor. As he greeted me, his expression changed. His wide eyes and tight lips showed his concern. Without hesitation, he delivered his diagnosis, 'My dear young lady, you have a goitre.' He picked up the phone and contacted a specialist, who agreed to see me in the morning.

Once the specialist finished examining me, he declared, 'Aminia, you have a thyroid condition with baffling complications.' I was confused, but more than that, I was terrified. My heartbeat hammered against my chest. I turned to my mother for support. Her face was white, and her eyes were closed tight to control the tears that glistened on her lashes. The specialist was a lovely man with a caring nature. His soothing voice relieved some of my tension as he said,

Waking to a Nightmare
Deceived by a Charming, Narcissist Paedophile

'Don't worry, young lady, we will get you all sorted and back to health in no time.'

His words comforted my mother a little. She put on a brave face and smiled at me, 'You'll be okay, darling. I'm confident you are in good hands, and I am right by your side.'

I met with Ivan that night, and after I told him about my diagnosis, he drew me close to him and kissed the top of my head, 'Aminia, I'm so sorry you are going through this. He stepped back and lifted my chin, 'Come now, show me your beautiful smile. We will get through this together.' He was my man, and our relationship was the only bright light in my darkness. His loving attention soothed my fear and comforted and distracted me from my health issues.

I was admitted to the hospital early the next day. My nerves jangled as the reality of being in a medical facility overwhelmed my senses.

Waking to a Nightmare
Deceived by a Charming, Narcissist Paedophile

It took some time before I received the proper treatment, as my condition swung erratically between overactive and underactive thyroid function. My energy swings had me feeling like I was riding on a rollercoaster, soaring up one moment and plummeting down the next. I was gripped with fear.

After careful deliberation, my team of dedicated specialists devised a treatment plan that held promise for my recovery. With the prescribed medication, I embarked on the journey towards regaining my health. And indeed, the progress was encouraging. I felt myself slowly returning to a state of well-being, and when my doctor gave me a positive examination result, I breathed a long sigh of relief.

During my time in the hospital, Ivan, who had once captured my heart with his devotion and care, only visited me twice. His presence was fleeting, and a certain restlessness seemed to consume him. When my mind questioned this, I slipped into despair and wondered whether my man had gone cold

Waking to a Nightmare
Deceived by a Charming, Narcissist Paedophile

towards me. But as was my way, I forgave him. How could I fault Ivan when I, too, longed to break free from the confines of the hospital walls and fly into the arms of my lover?

On the day of my discharge, I couldn't contain my excitement and performed a comical, awkward rendition of an Irish jig in my hospital room, much to the amusement of my fellow patients. Their laughter filled the room, creating a reprieve from the sombre atmosphere.

To my surprise and delight, Ivan was waiting to take me home. Soon, we resumed our relationship as though we had never been separated. Ivan's devotion and attentiveness convinced me that I was the love of his life. As I regained my strength, our bond deepened, and I was assured that we would face any challenges hand in hand.

Once I felt I could handle the demands of university, I enrolled to continue my teacher training. It was a period of

Waking to a Nightmare
Deceived by a Charming, Narcissist Paedophile

growth and self-discovery, both personally and professionally.

Upon graduating, I accepted a position at a church school while awaiting an opportunity to arise in the public education system. However, my time at the school took two disturbing turns. At the school assembly, the Deputy Principal, a nun, used a steel-edged ruler to strike one of my seven-year-old students across his knuckles. My blood ran cold, and my protest lept out of me, 'How dare you strike one of my students? He is only seven, and your disciplinary measure was over the top.' I believed my confrontation with her would cause my dismissal from the school. However, nothing came of it, and I continued teaching my class and enjoyed doing so.

A few days later, another incident shook me to my core. While on playground supervision, I noticed a young novice struggling with the gate latch leading from the priest's residence that adjoined the school grounds. She shed

Waking to a Nightmare
Deceived by a Charming, Narcissist Paedophile

uncontrollable tears as she attempted to open the gate. Moved by her distress, I rushed to her aid. Her hysterical sobbing and trembling body made me realise something awful had occurred. I put my arm around her waist and felt her tremors as I guided her to a secluded bench seat. After her sobs subsided a little, I urged her to tell me what had happened. At first, she was silent. My psychology lectures taught me that many children and adults go quiet after a traumatic experience.

The girl emitted a long shuddering sigh, then in hesitant sentences interlaced with sobs and poignant pauses, her words startled me. 'I hate cleaning the priest's residence because he makes me sit on his lap while he kisses and touches me. I hate him!' I couldn't believe what I was hearing.

The weight of this young girl's words hung between us. My heart ached for this novice who had experienced such a traumatic ordeal. She was no more than a child, about fifteen years old. I offered to accompany her while she reported what had happened to her. She jumped up and spat her words at me, 'No! I can't be thrown out of here. I… I'll have nowhere else to live.' She darted off.

That incident left an indelible mark on my mind and a lingering sense of helplessness. Being young and inexperienced, I grappled with the magnitude of the situation and the limitations of my ability to take immediate action. Guilt plagued my thoughts for days as I questioned whether I could have done more. I felt I had failed her. I never saw her again, and I can only hope she found the support and safety she needed to heal and move forward.

I shared this distressing incident with Ivan. He expressed his absolute horror and disgust at the perpetrator's actions. His empathy and concern for the young woman resonated with me, solidifying our bond. Our relationship continued to strengthen, and discussions of marriage became a natural progression.

Waking to a Nightmare
Deceived by a Charming, Narcissist Paedophile

Little did I know that Ivan's dark and sinister side would emerge, inflicting pain and suffering upon me that would far surpass anything I had ever experienced in my sheltered life. The realisation of this truth would unfold over time, shattering the illusions of our picture-perfect life and thrusting me into a nightmarish reality I never anticipated.

I LIKEN IVAN TO A SPIDER STALKING ITS PREY, POUNCING ON IT, AND SLOWLY DEVOURING IT.

Waking to a Nightmare
Deceived by a Charming, Narcissist Paedophile

CHAPTER 3

How did I fail to see the signs that had always been there? When you trick your mind into thinking someone is perfect for you, you ignore the warning red flags in front of you. You see everything through your rose-tinted glasses, so those red flags are invisible. And this is how it was for the inexperienced, starry-eyed me.

I left teaching and landed a lucrative job in the company I had worked for before attending university. There I met a new man. He was friendly, charming, and caring. This man's compassionate attention caused me to reassess the troubling doubts I had about Ivan. I removed those rose-coloured glasses and called quits on Ivan and our relationship—the joy of feeling free sent tingles through me. After returning home from a date with my new flame and kissing him goodnight, I was unaware that a trap was about to capture me in its jaws.

Waking to a Nightmare
Deceived by a Charming, Narcissist Paedophile

My mother met me as I walked through the door, 'Aminia, you must decide which man you want to be with! You know Ivan loves you and wants to marry you. I don't know what has gotten into you.' Caught off-guard, all the good things I had been feeling dissipated. My mother continued, 'Ivan is here. He is upset and very drunk. She held the tops of my arms and looked into my eyes, 'You know, Aminia, I think Ivan will be an excellent husband for you.'

My mother thought his love for me was real. She spoke of him as though the sun shone out of him. I doubted my feelings and believed my mother knew what was best for me.

Muffled voices drew me to the kitchen, where my father tried to sober Ivan. I must admit I was taken by surprise by Ivan's inebriated state. I sat at the far end of the table. Ivan lifted his bleary eyes towards me and pleaded, 'Please, Mite, come back to me.' Mite was the only endearing word he ever bestowed upon me. Appropriate, I now realise, because a

Waking to a Nightmare
Deceived by a Charming, Narcissist Paedophile

mite is a small annoying bug, and that is what I must have been to him.

I remained quiet while my mind whirled through many thoughts. After taking a few gulps of tea, Ivan stood and staggered around the table to me. I pulled away from his stinking breath. Dad ushered him into the spare room and put him to bed. That whole night, I churned over my thoughts and feelings. I had only met my new man three days ago and realised I knew little about him. On the other hand, Ivan was familiar to me, and when he engaged his charms, he always managed to lure me back into his trap. If only I had thrown away those glasses and faced his sinister tactics.

In the morning, Ivan apologised to my parents. Then he embraced me, sobbing into my hair, 'Please forgive me, Mite. I can do better. All I want is for us to be happy.' He dropped to one knee and proposed we get married soon. I was stunned. I heard my mother gasp, and when I looked

Waking to a Nightmare
Deceived by a Charming, Narcissist Paedophile

over at her, she was smiling and nodding her head, and I said, 'Okay, yes.'

Once again, Ivan manipulated me and used my mother to convince me he was sincere. For some time after, he showered me with loving attention. And I slipped right back into his web.

From the moment Ivan proposed, time threw me into a whirlwind of frantic preparation for our wedding and took my thoughts away from any concerns. A friend of our family was a jeweller who offered to make my rings for me. He and I collaborated on their design. I didn't know until later that he gave them to Ivan and announced they were his wedding gift to us. The engagement ring would later disappear under strange circumstances. Ivan was non-plussed about the missing ring and was not interested in helping me find it.

The day Ivan formally proposed, he took me for a drive and parked at a spot overlooking one of our favourite beaches. I don't remember what caused an argument, but I was crying.

Waking to a Nightmare
Deceived by a Charming, Narcissist Paedophile

As I tried to calm myself, Ivan laughed and wiped my tears away with his thumbs. 'The trouble with you, Mite, is you're too sensitive.'

Then he jumped out of the car and went to the boot, leaving me devastated and confused. When he returned, he had the engagement ring and a massive bunch of flowers. He professed his love for me and said, 'No silly little argument will ever cause us to part.' I later realised this was a part of Ivan's disarming narcissistic character.

After our wedding, Ivan enrolled in a university course to advance his career prospects. He loathed doing the required research and often asked me to do that. His favourite subject was child psychology. I remember a chilling statement he said to me, *'You can make a child believe anything. All you do is say it right and often enough until they believe it.'*

I would later be shocked when I knew what he did to his innocent young victims. He groomed our daughter from when she was a toddler, and he is still controlling her. And

Waking to a Nightmare
Deceived by a Charming, Narcissist Paedophile

he groomed me. For the most part, when we first married, Ivan was the perfect husband. His words and actions were loving and caring. But as time passed, his attitude towards me changed, and I described his lovemaking as "wham, bam, thank you, *mam*". There was no foreplay or enjoyment. One day, I questioned him about this change, and he said, 'You are a wife now, and I don't have to take the time to please you.' Why I stayed faithful is a mystery to me now. I can only put it down to my upbringing.

I helped him with his university assignments. He would take me to the library, hand me the notes of the assignment outline, and disappear. I remember looking around for him at the university one day. I found him smoking and drinking with students at the canteen. I was angry and told him that I would stop helping him. I also reminded him that I did the lion's share of his research. 'Ah, there you go again, Mite, overreacting! We are discussing an assignment due for assessment next week.'

Waking to a Nightmare
Deceived by a Charming, Narcissist Paedophile

He was an A1 manipulator.

During this time, Ivan often went to other people's places to study (always women). One night, he came home after midnight. I confronted him. 'Where have you been? I have been worried about you.'

He told me that the car had broken down and that he had to wait for Roadside Service. I asked him why he didn't phone me.

'I didn't want to disturb the lady I was studying with because she would have gone to bed.'

I didn't believe Ivan. When he tried to start the car, it would have only been a short time after he said goodnight to her! And there were no mobile phones then, so how did he call for assistance?

I put these questions to Ivan. He grabbed my arm tight and glared down at me. I could see pure rage sparking in his eyes. 'You spit the dummy like that all the time! You have no faith

Waking to a Nightmare
Deceived by a Charming, Narcissist Paedophile

in me. Your jealousy will destroy our relationship!' I could feel his spittle hitting my face and the pain of his long fingers digging into my arms. Fear gripped me.

He began staying out late more often. On one occasion, he didn't come home at all, and I was beside myself, thinking he had met with an accident. He justified his actions by saying he was studying with his best mate, who asked him to join him for a drink. 'I couldn't drive home because I had too much to drink. Surely you can understand that, can't you? You have an evil imagination!' he yelled as he stood over me. I didn't dare question why he didn't phone me.

A couple of days later, I was at the library when I met his mate. I commented on his and Ivan's overnight study and drinking spree. Ivan's mate looked confused. 'You must be mistaken; I was at home that night, and besides, Ivan hasn't been to my place for months.'

Waking to a Nightmare
Deceived by a Charming, Narcissist Paedophile

My heart burned, and hot tears threatened to fall. Ivan was spiralling out of control. I wish I had known then that I was dealing with a narcissist.

I remember a chilling statement Ivan made after finishing his degree. 'You can make a child believe anything you want them to believe. All you need to do is say it the right way and often enough, and they will do or say whatever you want them to.' This raised considerable concerns in me, and I voiced these. He laughed and said, Here you go again, Aminia, taking things the wrong way. He grabbed my arm and twisted me towards him, 'Why do you always read things into stuff that is not real?'

I tried to pull free of him, 'Let me go; you are hurting me!'

He snarled, 'It's your fault I hurt you because you frustrate me so much. It's your insecurities that push me over the edge.' Later, I would understand how this attitude supported his narcissistic and paedophilic tendencies.

Waking to a Nightmare
Deceived by a Charming, Narcissist Paedophile

His unsettling confession was the catalyst for me to tear my rosy glasses off. I could see where my nightmare took its full-fledged sinister shape. He disregarded all my suspicions and tried to make me feel sorry for my *"misguided accusations."* 'It is your insecurities that give weight to your silly ideas,' he told me.

Yes, I did feel insecure, but mostly I felt unloved. And yes, it was silly to believe in him for so long. At this point, my mind was in turmoil. My thoughts tumbled around like clothes in a dryer, and I didn't know where the off switch was.

Sometimes, I would rise above his accusations. He seemed to sense when I began to feel strong. Then, he would use his quiet reasoning voice, and his criticisms of me were coached in his liquid, smooth voice. This tactic affected my mind, and I berated myself for being such a lousy wife.

Waking to a Nightmare
Deceived by a Charming, Narcissist Paedophile

'Was I going mad?' Where had the happy Aminia gone? Had someone else moved into her mind and body?' The answer to this is a resounding YES!

During the initial years of my marriage, I enjoyed much of it. Ivan and I liked picnics, hiking through the bush, and travelling to exciting places.

I recall when Ivan, his mother, and I walked along a popular hikers' bush track. I moved ahead while they chatted behind me. It was a beautiful spring day, and many people were soaking it up. True to my friendly, outgoing nature, I interacted with some passersby.

Later, Ivan expressed how shocked he and his mother were by my behaviour with strangers. He confessed that her words triggered feelings of insecurity and jealousy within him. 'You know, Aminia, you are so naïve. For your protection, I should **lock you in a gilded cage.**'

Waking to a Nightmare
Deceived by a Charming, Narcissist Paedophile

NARCISSISTS MUST HAVE COMPLETE CONTROL OVER THEIR VICTIMS.

Waking to a Nightmare
Deceived by a Charming, Narcissist Paedophile

CHAPTER 4

Divorce was not an easy option in those days. The red flags kept popping up, but I pushed them aside and ignored their warnings. Instead, I slipped my rose-coloured glasses back on and immersed myself in my work, and so the actions of my narcissistic husband as he wreaked havoc on the lives of those around him went unnoticed. In my defence, he was clever at keeping me in the dark. Or, if I questioned his actions, he would accuse me of having an evil mind.

Every one of our friends and acquaintances said I was so lucky to be married to such a wonderful and charming man. I convinced myself that they were right and that, as Ivan often pointed out, my stupid insecurities caused me to doubt him.

Ivan was offered the role of a school community liaison officer and took it. He encouraged me to get involved in the communities in which we lived, and now I know that made

Waking to a Nightmare
Deceived by a Charming, Narcissist Paedophile

him look more legitimate. I don't know how often I heard women say, 'Oh, Ivan is such a lovely man. You are a lucky woman.' This man didn't only hoodwink me.

I began to doubt myself, so I decided to ignore my misgivings. I didn't complain when Ivan stayed out late. I believed he was doing what he claimed, implementing new support programs for vulnerable young women teachers working in remote areas.

In the meantime, I was busy being the dutiful wife, keeping house and entertaining his colleagues who frequently visited our home. To the outside world, we had a perfect marriage. I put on my happy face in public while I dismissed my emotional inner dialogue and convinced myself that Ivan was right and I was being paranoid.

I fell pregnant two years on, and Ivan didn't seem that rapt. He spent more time away *"working on projects"*. As the baby inside me grew, Ivan was barely there as a husband, and I felt isolated and cried often.

Waking to a Nightmare
Deceived by a Charming, Narcissist Paedophile

One day, I summoned the courage to tell him how I felt. Ivan took me in his arms, professed his love for me and promised to try to lessen his workload. For a few weeks, he stayed home and was more attentive to me. I drifted on a blissful cloud as this masterful narcissist drew me further into his web of deceit.

Soon, another young female teacher needed Ivan's help. This gave him the excuse to stay away often and for long hours into the night. I ignored my pounding heart and tricked myself into admiring him for his dedication to his career.

Towards the end of my pregnancy, I gave up work. Ivan often reminded me that he was now the only breadwinner and had to work harder and longer hours to provide for me and the child I carried.

The Narcissist knew how to play me like a fish on a hook. Ivan was a master at reading my moods and would lure me with loving words when I would pull away from him. Our acquaintances, especially the women, admired him, so I must have been the problem. In hindsight, those women also fell for his beguiling ways because he convinced them to believe in him. The master manipulator was at his best, cleverly disguising his true nature.

My daughter's birth led me into a whole new ordeal. Her birthing was extremely difficult and lengthy. I was consumed by severe pain. The nurse ordered Ivan to leave the birthing room. Later, he told me he was terrified. He heard the nurse calling the doctor five times to come and attend to me, as I was in difficulty, and they could not help me. After some time, the hospital's registrar doctor burst through the door, and his contorted, concerned expression did not settle my mind. By then, the pain was so intense that my thoughts were chaotic.

Because it was New Year's Eve, my obstetrician was at a party and had imbibed too much alcohol to drive, let alone assist in a difficult birthing. The panicked actions of the midwives around me seemed to seep into my body; all I

Waking to a Nightmare
Deceived by a Charming, Narcissist Paedophile

wanted was for the pain to end. As the last of my energy seeped from my body, I felt myself drifting into pure whiteness. A sudden sharp noise drew me back into the mayhem as the doctor injected me with some medication. But my condition worsened; my breathing stopped. Somehow, I made it back.

Maybe fate still wanted me here to do what I would all these years on…to tell my story, hoping it would help others.

I woke the following day with searing pain gripping my body with every tiny move I made. But more concerning was my worry about my baby. I had decided to name her Katherine, after my grandmother. I was sure she had died. I curled my body into a ball to stop the physical pain that tore through me and to alleviate the mental anguish of losing my precious baby. Vaguely, I was aware of people around me, but I wanted to scream at them, 'Leave me be. Why didn't you let me die?'

Waking to a Nightmare
Deceived by a Charming, Narcissist Paedophile

Later in the afternoon, a young nurse came to administer my medication. 'Have you seen your beautiful little Poppet?' he asked. I sobbed and buried my head under the bed covers. *Was he joking, or maybe confused? My baby was dead.* My anguish pulled a tight band around my head, and my surgery caused searing, sharp pains to grab at my abdomen. This empathetic man touched me lightly on my shoulder, 'I'll be back soon.' he declared as my heavy eyes closed.

The sound of a lift door opening brought my attention back to my pain. A humidity crib bumped the side of my bed. With gentle hands, the nurse picked my daughter up and laid her on the bed beside me. 'Hi, Aminia. My name is Tom. We will count your baby girl's fingers and toes, and you will see she is perfect.'

My baby is alive! I held her in my arms as we checked her out. 'She is perfect!' I declared, shedding tears of joy.

Waking to a Nightmare
Deceived by a Charming, Narcissist Paedophile

Tom nodded, 'Yes, she is, and she is a favourite in the nursery because she is so cute.' I'm sure he said this to make me feel better.

It was two long days after Kathy's birth before I could feed her. Although I was sorry, I couldn't breastfeed her because I was still recovering, and my medication would have harmed her. My wonderful nurse hooked his arm around me to help me sit up. With great care, he positioned pillows around me for support. He lowered my child into my arms as though delivering a precious parcel. Yes, my baby was beautiful and perfect.

Little did I know that something sinister and unthinkable lay waiting to emerge in this child's future, twisting her perspective on life and shattering our relationship.

After an extended stay in the hospital, Ivan picked Kathy and me up and drove us home. My parents waited for us in our apartment, and I remember thinking that if they smiled any wider, their faces would crack. My husband changed Kathy's

Waking to a Nightmare
Deceived by a Charming, Narcissist Paedophile

nappy and picked her up, cradling her over his shoulder as my mother snapped a photo. **'She is mine.'** He declared in his authoritative voice. Those ominous words now make me shiver.

'Of course, she is yours,' I laughed, unaware of the sinister intent to obliterate Kathy and my relationship years later.

Ivan's time at home lengthened, and I was hopeful things between us would change for the better. But my heart ached as all his attention was focused on his daughter. As I think about those early days, I wonder…was Ivan already scheming to twist our daughter's mind so that he could control her, too?

At that point in our relationship, I did not know the evil that lurked in Ivan's paedophile soul. My mind could not even begin to comprehend what horrors lay ahead.

Waking to a Nightmare
Deceived by a Charming, Narcissist Paedophile

ARE PAEDOPHILES BORN THAT WAY, OR DOES SOMETHING TRIGGER THEM, CAUSING THEIR MIND TO WARP? I DID NOT KNOW.

Waking to a Nightmare
Deceived by a Charming, Narcissist Paedophile

CHAPTER 5

When Kathy was only two months old, our family of three moved to a small town on the western slopes about 200 kilometres north of Sydney. With each passing day, Ivan became even more obsessed with his daughter. That phrase, **'she is mine**,' would come back to haunt me. But for now, his actions didn't raise unsettling feelings in me... I just thought he was a top-notch, loving father.

When my daughter was nearly two years old, I gave birth to my son, Mitchell—a vastly different experience. Without any drama, he slid into this world. However, the day I brought him home from the hospital remains imprinted on my memory. Our dog suffered from a tick and was quite ill; Ivan focused on the dog. Being a new mother with hormones firing through my body, I was sad and vulnerable. I confronted Ivan for not being interested in his son, to which he replied with venom in his words, 'My dog is dying, which is more important right now! Your son has you to take care of him!'

How could a father say that? And how could he ignore his baby son? I felt devastated and alone. I snapped! Hot tears flowed from me as my words lashed out at Ivan. I did not doubt myself this time when he turned my words back at me. He walked away. I began packing my bags and the children's belongings. I wanted to run far from this dispassionate man and never look back.

When Ivan saw me packing to leave, he hauled me into his arms and begged me to stay. Once again, The Narcissist used his devious manipulation skills, sighting the needs of my children, to keep me from doing what I wanted: **to run and not look back!** I caved in and stayed. After all, where would I go? I knew Ivan would have followed me to the ends of the Earth to retrieve his daughter. How could I walk away from my little girl? That was not an option. My heart felt tight and

Waking to a Nightmare
Deceived by a Charming, Narcissist Paedophile

hot, and I felt ill. Feeling alone and helpless, I uttered static words of apology.

As time progressed, it became apparent that Ivan showed little attention to our son when nobody else was present. The dog incident wasn't a one-time thing; Ivan's ambivalence towards his son continued and worsened. Ivan put on a show of caring for Mitch only in the presence of other people. His centre of attention was always Kathy.

As I write this, I am reminded of something that may have shaped Ivan's warped thinking. There were three boys in Ivan's family. His mother was staying with us, and she was a heavy drinker. Slurring her words, she told me that she didn't like her firstborn because he had altered her body, and she didn't like Ivan because he was supposed to be a girl. I wonder whether Ivan's besotted behaviour towards Kathy was due to this attitude of his mother. It played out during my time with Ivan because his mother and father paid little attention to Mitch while lavishing Kathy with compliments

Waking to a Nightmare
Deceived by a Charming, Narcissist Paedophile

and unbridled attention. Perhaps this led to Ivan's warped way with girls.

Mitch was a poor sleeper, and his crying tore through me throughout the night. Ivan yelled at me and demanded I keep him quiet. I often took Mitch out of the room and attempted to soothe him; sleep was a luxury that illuded me for most nights. I moved through my days like a zombie, snatching random moments of rest during the day. But this was not enough to revive my energy or peace of mind.

Ivan's attitude towards Mitch and my lack of sleep pushed me towards the edge one night. Mitch cried non-stop. No matter what I did, I was not able to quieten him. Ivan shouted at me, 'Keep that bastard kid quiet!'

In a moment of despair, I almost lost it. I gathered Mitch up and considered throwing him at the wall. Instead, I dropped him beside me on the bed and screamed at Ivan, 'You have got to take him so I can sleep. I need sleep!' Ivan's face was blood red, and sparks flew from his eyes, but he took Mitch.

Waking to a Nightmare
Deceived by a Charming, Narcissist Paedophile

I tossed and turned as guilty thoughts whirled through my troubled mind. Sleep alluded me, and I berated myself, 'Aminia, you are a terrible mother to even think of doing something that would hurt your child!'.

When I changed Mitch's nappy in the morning, his bottom was bleeding from many weeping sores. I packed him in the car and drove to see my doctor, who had birthed him. My doctor and I became good friends. I called him Doc. He always gave me his last appointment of the day, and we would have a great yarn over a glass of wine. Doc once said about Mitch, 'This little fella makes me clucky.' I laughed. He had five girls and was happily married.

As I entered Doc's consulting room, he noticed my stressed attitude and said, 'Aminia, what on Earth is wrong with you?' I blabbered about Mitch not sleeping and his bleeding bottom. He undid his nappy and stated, 'I know what is wrong with him. He is allergic to the lactose of milk.'

Waking to a Nightmare
Deceived by a Charming, Narcissist Paedophile

I went straight to the chemist's shop and bought lactose-free baby formula. Ah, bliss! That night, Mitch slept soundly and every other night after that. During the day, he was a happy, bouncing baby boy. I thought, *Surely now Ivan will warm towards Mitch*. But no! He continued to give him little attention. However, his obsession with his daughter was growing.

Ivan mainly worked with young female teachers in our area and often came home late. My mother's advice regarding **jealousy is a curse** made me feel I was the problem and, therefore, I was destroying our relationship, so I pushed aside my fears and doubts. Many times, I reprimanded myself for my suspicious feelings and then picked up those rose-coloured glasses.

Ivan was quick to make new friends with the mothers of young daughters. Maybe that was his way of getting close to young girls. This thought reminded me of a disturbing statement Ivan had made. We sat on our back porch,

Waking to a Nightmare
Deceived by a Charming, Narcissist Paedophile

enjoying a glass of wine and a snack. The town basketball court ran beside our backyard. A group of girls aged ten to twelve were practising their skills. They were wearing their basketball uniforms. All Ivan's attention was on them as he took a long sip of his beer and declared, 'I love watching them bouncing around in their short skirts. **Those girls turn me on!**'

I was stunned. My mouth dropped open, and for a moment, words would not form in my dry mouth. I felt disgusted. Then these words flew out of me, 'Ivan, what you just said is most inappropriate.'

With a smirk twisting his face, Ivan said, 'Don't be so stupid; I'm just joking.'

Years later, when Ivan and I were working at another school, the yardman told me he was alarmed by what Ivan said to him. He and Ivan were having a beer after school hours, and a group of girls were practising their basketball techniques

Waking to a Nightmare
Deceived by a Charming, Narcissist Paedophile

on the school basketball court. Ivan used the exact phrase,

'Those girls turn me on.'

Bile filled my mouth as I asked the yardman whether he had said anything to Ivan about this inappropriate comment, and he said, 'Hell no! He is my boss, and I need that job.'

A LEOPARD DOES NOT CHANGE HIS SPOTS.

Waking to a Nightmare
Deceived by a Charming, Narcissist Paedophile

CHAPTER 6

We moved to another remote school several kilometres away on the Western side of NSW's Great Dividing Range. My time was now spent doing occasional relief teaching. The rest of my time was spent caring for my daughter and son. The school owned a bus, and Ivan often asked me to accompany him on excursions. He only wanted me there because I got on well with Indigenous students. For me, they weren't any different than my children. I ensured they felt comfortable and happy and often invited them to my home.

I joined the playgroup in the town that catered only for white children. I began doing activities designed to interest the older children. This caught the attention of the playgroup committee. One of the women approached me and informed me, 'The other mothers and I have noticed how good you are with our kids, and they have asked me to inquire whether you would develop a preschool for the three to five-year-

Waking to a Nightmare
Deceived by a Charming, Narcissist Paedophile

olds.' There was only one preschool in town, which was run at the Indigenous Mission School, so white children could not attend.

I didn't have to think about it for long as my empathetic nature kicked into gear, 'Yes, I would love to do that. I have one proviso: it will be open to Indigenous and white children.' To my delight, the mothers agreed. After some brainstorming, I devised a strategy to put before the committee. 'This is my proposal; I will do it on the condition that I will train four women as preschool teachers: two Caucasian and two Indigenous women.' All the mothers agreed, and I restrained from doing my Irish gig on the spot…such was my delight.

The initial idea was that the Preschool would be held in the same venue as the playgroup. However, the people in charge of the hall flipped when they learned that Indigenous children would be invited to attend. They declared they would not allow me to have the Preschool on their premises

Waking to a Nightmare
Deceived by a Charming, Narcissist Paedophile

if I allowed 'blacks' to attend. I responded, 'I always thought your organisation espoused to be non-sectarian and, therefore, would welcome all into this hall.' They turned their backs and walked away.

I wasn't going to let this stop me. With the support of the four women, I was training to run the preschool, and a few other mothers, I decided to organise a grand opening of the preschool at the local park. It was a great success! I was speechless when I saw the number of white and Indigenous mothers and some fathers who turned up. But best of all, was the interaction between the kids. People brought delicious food, and everybody had a great time. Reporters from the local newspaper showed up and documented the event. They wrote an article accompanied by excellent photos. When Ivan and I separated, he took all my cherished mementos of that magical day, including photos and newspaper clippings. As I write this, I feel a lump in my throat, and my eyes sting from unshed tears.

Waking to a Nightmare
Deceived by a Charming, Narcissist Paedophile

Something else motivated me to move towards integrating the Indigenous and white communities. On the first day of school after the Christmas break, a group of Indigenous children from the Mission School were lined up outside the gate of "The Big School" (The Big School was the local name for this Central Public School, which catered for kindergarten children aged 5 to Year 10, aged 15). It was apparent the children were scared. I was determined to do something to help them transition from their smaller, familiar mission school. The government of the day decreed that all the Indigenous children, from the start of their third schooling year, had to attend a public school.

My heart skipped a beat as I watched these obviously scared young children with their eyes downcast while they scraped their feet in the dirt. I felt I had to do something. I approached the principal of the Central School to obtain his permission to invite the Indigenous children from the Mission School and our Preschool to attend anything that

Waking to a Nightmare
Deceived by a Charming, Narcissist Paedophile

would interest them, such as visiting shows, films, special days, and, where possible, attending some aged-appropriate classes. I believed that helping these scared young Indigenous children feel more welcome would make their transition to 'The Big School' easier and reduce their anxiety. To my delight, the principal agreed, and it worked.

Soon after arriving in this town, I became close friends with Keith and his wife. They owned a large sheep station not far from our home. I was delighted to discover that Keith and I had a mutual interest in local history. By then, I had already begun guiding the children in "The Big School" to collect verbal and written historical information to be added to the community newspaper.

While sitting around a fire at Keith's place, he and I discussed establishing a town museum. I put an article in the school mag to gauge the community's interest. The response was positive, and Keith and I danced around his firepit, flinging our arms up and shouting, 'We did it, we did it!

Waking to a Nightmare
Deceived by a Charming, Narcissist Paedophile

On a non-school day, I was home with my children when two Indigenous men arrived in my driveway. 'Miss (all white women were called *Miss* whether you were single or married), we have something we think you will be interested in putting in the museum.'

These men were strangers to me, and after a brief hesitation, my curiosity drew me to follow them out to their van. When they opened the back of it, my eyes boggled at the vast collection of indigenous artifacts inside. They ranged from large grinding dishes and grinding stones to tiny spearheads. One of the men reached into the van and pulled out a cardboard box. Inside was a prised piece, a complete Widow's Cap! This was rare because, mostly, there were only partial specimens of these. The Widow's Cap was made of Gipson, a type of cement found around that area. The woman had to wear the cap for a year or until it broke. These caps were heavy and uncomfortable, and so the widows broke them. The Widow's Cap I held in my hands was in

Waking to a Nightmare
Deceived by a Charming, Narcissist Paedophile

perfect condition. Inside, it still had some of the hair of the woman who had worn it. It took all my effort not to burst into my famous Irish jig.' I heard that our National Museum didn't possess a total cap. (I never did find the time to check on that.)

The two men were excited by my reaction. Finally, when I found my voice, I asked, 'What do you want to do with your precious collection?'

'Since we were young boys, we have been collecting these. When we heard you were establishing a museum in town, we thought we'd like to give them to you so you can exhibit them there.'

I placed my hands over my heart and said, 'I am honoured by your offer. This is a mind-blowing collection! I honestly have never seen anything like it.'

Waking to a Nightmare
Deceived by a Charming, Narcissist Paedophile

I offered them two options: to 'gift' the artifacts to the museum or donate them while retaining the right of ownership. Of course, they chose the second option.

That same day, I took the precious Widow's cap in its plain cardboard box to the bank and informed the manager that I had a deposit to go into the bank's safe. 'What on Earth are you asking, Aminia? We don't take deposits to keep in our safe!' he declared. The manager was astonished when I carefully removed the Widow's cap from the cardboard box. Without further objection, he placed it in his safe.

Keith and I were pumped. However, we then had the task of cataloguing all those precious articles. In one of Keith's sheds, we lined up trestle tables borrowed from organisations all over town. It was a scorching day. We started laying all the artifacts on the tables early in the morning, but some had to be put on the tables outside. As we worked throughout the day, we were so busy and oblivious

Waking to a Nightmare
Deceived by a Charming, Narcissist Paedophile

to the hot sun on us that we both suffered from heatstroke! I had to spend overnight in the local hospital.

I thoroughly enjoyed my time in that community. However, one of my greatest regrets is that I couldn't attend the museum opening. Ivan applied for a move, and I had to leave with him. The preschool is still running today, although it is now housed in its purpose-built premises.

A few years later, while living in another town, the local Lion's Club invited me to their meeting. As I entered the door, I was surprised when I was greeted by two people who had travelled hundreds of kilometres from that western town to attend a ceremony to induct me as an Honorary Life Member of the Lion's Club. Word had gone out about the work I had done for their town, not only as the driving force behind the establishment of the all-inclusive Preschool but also my joint work with Keith in starting the establishment of the museum.

Waking to a Nightmare
Deceived by a Charming, Narcissist Paedophile

Luckily, When Ivan removed all my mementos after we separated, he did not know the combination to my safe, and I still have the Lion's Club letter and badge.

Waking to a Nightmare
Deceived by a Charming, Narcissist Paedophile

CHAPTER 7

A new job – a new school purposely built for Indigenous children. I was the librarian, taught arts and crafts, and was a relieving teacher. Kathy started her schooling and was the only white child for four months until two more white children enrolled.

While teaching my class, I noticed a lady striding up the path carrying a large briefcase. I was surprised when she asked for me. The Department of Education had sent her to talk to me about establishing an Indigenous preschool like the one I had set up before. She pulled a wad of papers from her briefcase for me to sign. The job came with a lucrative salary and all the help I required. I asked for some time to consider this offer. Ivan was delighted. He picked me up and twirled me around his office. 'You must do it. You do realise it will be good for both of us.'

Waking to a Nightmare
Deceived by a Charming, Narcissist Paedophile

After accepting the job, I was informed that I would be training an Indigenous lady named Jan. I think Ivan recommended her. When I moved on, she was to take over my preschool teacher and administrative role. Instead of spending time with me learning about running the preschool and training as an early childhood teacher, she spent most of her time with Ivan in his office during school hours and, later, well into the night.

When I questioned Ivan, he told me he was training her to be the school office manager. As time passed, Ivan and Jan spent more and more time together. He encouraged Kathy and Jan's daughter to become good friends.

Until then, Ivan was the first to go to bed while I tucked the children in and read them stories. After Kathy and Mitch dosed off, I did household chores and preparations for my next day of teaching. Ivan began taking long walks at around midnight. When I questioned him about this unusual behaviour, he said, 'I get clearer about tackling any issues

Waking to a Nightmare
Deceived by a Charming, Narcissist Paedophile

that have come up during the day. But why are you bloody well questioning me about what I do?'

While I was frustrated with the lack of interest Jan gave in her support position to me – I must admit I found it easier to implement what was needed without her. Within a short time, I called meetings with interested parents, and a working committee was formed. Jan was supposed to attend but was seconded by Ivan to work with him - on what was always a mystery.

During this time, my house phone rang. It was a call for Ivan, who was still at the school. I ran to let him know about the call. At his office door, I stopped short. Ivan was cuddling Jan and whispering into her ear. All colour drained from his face when he noticed me. He stepped away from her, then stuttered, 'What are you doing here?'

I responded, 'More to the point, what did I just witness?' He told me Jan was upset about something that had happened, and he was only consoling her.

Waking to a Nightmare
Deceived by a Charming, Narcissist Paedophile

Jan's daughter was a few months younger than Kathy. Ivan often insisted I look after the girls while Jan and he worked together at the school. At this stage, I did not know that Ivan was having an affair with Jan! It was convenient for this deceitful pair to have Jan's daughter sleep overnight at our house a few times a week.

Arriving home late at night, Ivan often insisted he needed to kiss the girls goodnight. I questioned him about the length of time he always took with them. After all, they were only five years old and had school the next day. He dismissed my concerns, stating that he was either telling or reading them a story and that I should spend time with Mitch or prepare for my classes the next day.

This NARCISSIST PHILANDERER was my boss.

A couple of days later, I took my son to the doctor in the nearest town, 72 kilometres away. When I was returning, I saw Jan speeding towards us. The road was a narrow, one-vehicle road built high over a floodplain. It had dirt sidings

Waking to a Nightmare
Deceived by a Charming, Narcissist Paedophile

for vehicles to pull over and allow others to pass. Jan was driving a larger car than mine with a solid iron bull-bar on the front. She planted her foot on the accelerator and came straight at me. My reaction was fast. Whenever confronted with a dangerous situation, I have always remained calm. My instincts switched on. I swerved down a siding and zigzagged through the trees. Before me, I spired a ramp, swung the steering wheel, and returned to the road. Then my nerves kicked into gear. I stopped the car, gulped in several breaths, jumped out, grabbed Mitch into my shaking arms, held him tight, and kissed his face, waking him from a deep sleep. His startled little face puckered, and he cried. To this day, I believe that on that day, a higher power had looked over me and my son, helping me to steady my hands on the steering wheel while guiding me through those trees.

As I turned into my driveway, all calmness left me. I slumped over the steering wheel and drew several deep breaths to settle my nerves. I grabbed Mitch from his car seat, ran to

Waking to a Nightmare
Deceived by a Charming, Narcissist Paedophile

the school, and entered Ivan's office. His eyes boggled when I confronted him with my high-pitched, shaking voice. He came from behind his desk, slammed the door, and grabbed my upper arms. 'Calm down, Aminia. You are acting strange. And I think you are exaggerating and mistaken.'

'Mistaken! Exaggerating! How could you say such a thing? Do you think I would make this up?'

He emitted a strange laugh and again said, 'Calm down. I will talk to Jan and ask her what happened. I'm sure there is some explanation.'

The blood ran from my head; my knees shook as I sunk into the nearest chair. He walked out of his office and left me slumped there. Every part of my body shook as I tried to understand his reaction.

The next afternoon, I tidied the books in the school library while Mitch played with his toys on the floor. I heard Jan yelling at Ivan in his office. I did not desire to be anywhere

Waking to a Nightmare
Deceived by a Charming, Narcissist Paedophile

near this woman. I picked Mitch up and headed to my house that adjoined the schoolyard. As I entered the gate, I put Mitch down and took his hand. Without warning, Jan sprang at me like a savage dog and clawed at my face.

My father, a champion boxer in his platoon during World War II, taught me some valuable boxing moves, and in that instant, they kicked in. I punched Jan. She fell to the ground. I swept Mitch up and sprinted into the house.

Through my back window, I saw Ivan sprinting across our lawn. He had seen Jan chasing after me and followed her. After witnessing what had happened, he helped Jan stand and supported her to return to the school office. Around thirty minutes later, Ivan entered our backdoor. He appeared to be ashamed of what had happened and went about making a cuppa to settle my nerves.

The next day, a horrible sight accosted my eyes. Jan was punching my screaming three-year-old son. My ire rose, causing a taste of bile in my mouth as I raced to Mitch and

Waking to a Nightmare
Deceived by a Charming, Narcissist Paedophile

shouted at Jan. She took off. I gathered Mitch into a tight hug and ran to Ivan. Both Mitch and I were sobbing. Ivan asked what had happened. 'Jan belted our son!'

'What!' He exclaimed, then changed his voice into a soothing, calm tone, 'Now, come on, Aminia. I'm sure you are overreacting. You have it in for Jan. Heaven knows why. Now settle down, and I will take care of this.'

I was shaken to the core. He completely dismissed me, as always! I knew what I had seen. Jan, the woman who had attacked me, was now venting her anger upon our small child, yet Ivan defended her and dismissed my concerns, accusing me of overreacting. This was absurd, and it had to stop!

Now, I knew it was up to me to protect my family. I returned to my house, phoned the Area Director of Education and demanded a meeting with him. He told me he was busy. Mustering all my fury and courage, I snarled, 'If you do not

Waking to a Nightmare
Deceived by a Charming, Narcissist Paedophile

call a meeting right now, blood will most likely be on your hands!' The Area Director agreed to meet with me.

When I told Ivan about the meeting, he was furious and demanded I phone and cancel it.

I could feel the fire in my cheeks and the sparks in my eyes. I was the lioness protecting her cub. I snarled into Ivan's face, 'I WILL NOT DO THAT!

Ivan also insisted he attend the meeting, so I phoned my father and asked him to look after the children. My mum was away on a golfing trip.

On the way to the meeting, Ivan begged me not to say anything about his affair with Jan. Affair! There it was… his confession. I was not afraid to upset him anymore. My children's safety outweighed any of his needs. 'I will say whatever I need to ensure my children's safety.' Ivan pulled himself into a brooding ball with his arms crossed over his body and stared out the window. He never spoke another word while I drove the two-hour trip to the meeting.

WHEN FACING THE STRENGTH OF A PROTECTIVE MOTHER, THIS NARCISSIST COWERED.

Waking to a Nightmare
Deceived by a Charming, Narcissist Paedophile

CHAPTER 8

'Please do not tell anyone...'

I stopped the car in the parking area and glanced at this poor excuse for a man who was not a caring father or supportive husband. He grabbed my arm and begged, 'Please, Aminia, don't tell anyone about Jan and me.' I sat rigid in my seat and gripped the steering wheel until my knuckles turned white. My throat felt tight as I stared out the car window. Ivan was focused only on saving his precious reputation.

I fixed my eyes on the windscreen and drew every ounce of courage and disdain for Ivan into every word, 'I will say whatever is necessary to ensure my children's safety. And if your head rolls in the process, so be it.' Again, the mother lioness's claws were out. My only concern was the safety of my cubs, and nothing nor anybody was going to stand in my way. Ivan physically cowered in the face of my conviction and followed me with his head lowered like a chastised pup.

Waking to a Nightmare
Deceived by a Charming, Narcissist Paedophile

While we waited in the reception area, we did not speak to each other. Soon, we were ushered into an office. The District Inspector of Schools, The Area Director of Education, and our Local School Inspector sat behind a large desk. I was directed to sit on the other side of the desk, and Ivan was told to sit in the corner. He sat with his head down and hands folded in his lap like a naughty boy summoned to the principal's office.

Without any preamble, The Area Director asked me why I felt this meeting was urgent. I told them what Jan had done to Mitch and me. Even though I did not say anything about Ivan having an affair with Jan, I am sure these wise men read between the lines.

First, I was asked whether I would continue my work towards establishing the preschool. 'No, I will not because I am concerned about my children's safety, especially my son's. That is more important to me than any job!' Nothing would sway me from my resolve to keep my children safe.

Waking to a Nightmare
Deceived by a Charming, Narcissist Paedophile

Still, these men were persistent. They suggested ways to keep Mitch and me safe from another attack. One of the men declared that I could get a restraining order from the police. I shook my head and uttered a derisive sigh. 'That is a crazy idea. The nearest Police Station is fifty kilometres from our home, and the road is dirt and very dangerous! That woman could do us much harm before the police arrived.'

The Local School Inspector said, 'I have a granny flat that you and your children could occupy, and the children could go to a school in that town. Then you could drive to your present school and continue setting up the new preschool.' I was astonished at their naivety and stifled a sigh before reminding them that Jan would sooner or later come across my children and me because that was her shopping town. Not to mention that I would still be in danger of more attacks from her.

I had zero confidence in their ridiculous ideas and stood firm in my conviction to ensure my children's safety. I didn't care

Waking to a Nightmare
Deceived by a Charming, Narcissist Paedophile

about my job, my husband's position, or even the friendships I had formed.

In the final minutes of the meeting, the Aboriginal Liaison Officer was called to attend. After listening to a brief recap of the issues, his eyes opened wide, and the urgency in his voice drew everyone's attention. 'Get them out of there immediately! That woman, Jan, is dangerous and will either harm them or, even worse, kill them! Our records contain serious reports about her aggression against other people.'

Ivan and I were asked to sit outside while these men in suits discussed the situation.

When we were called back into the meeting, the Area Director asked whether we had anywhere we could go where we would be safe. This is the only time Ivan spoke. Until then, he had sat silent, looking like a small boy summoned to the principal's office after a misdemeanour. He stood and moved to stand beside me. His head was bowed, and he still held his hands nestled in front of him like a choir boy! His

Waking to a Nightmare
Deceived by a Charming, Narcissist Paedophile

voice was no more than a whisper as he began to speak. 'Um, ah, I have an uncle who has a farm with two houses. I think he would let us stay there.' Ivan was directed to use the secretary's phone outside the room. When he returned, he reported that his uncle affirmed that we could use the spare house for as long as needed.' I never knew what Ivan said to his uncle about the situation. He most likely lied, making sure he was seen as the victim.

The Aboriginal Liaison Officer said, 'I think I have the solution. I have a friend who is the principal of a school near where Aminia's family will now live. He has been trying to secure a move back into this area because he has a farm about 30 kilometres from the school Ivan will vacate. I will phone him.' He left the room. When he returned, he affirmed that his friend was delighted with the prospect of returning to his farm. From then on, things moved fast—removalists for both families were organised and paid for by the Department of Education.

Waking to a Nightmare
Deceived by a Charming, Narcissist Paedophile

When the meeting ended, it was close to 6 p.m. One of the Inspectors asked where we would stay that night. I told him I'd drive home to begin sorting and packing. One of the suits questioned whether that was wise. I assured him I felt safe because my father was staying with us.

After the exhausting meeting, the trip home was quiet. Again, I drove while Ivan cowered in the passenger seat. No words were spoken between us during the entire trip. I don't know where Ivan slept that night. At daybreak, I began packing and sorting some of our possessions.

After our evening meal, we were disturbed by a pounding on the door. My father answered it. Jan swung a lethal weapon at him - a crowbar! Dad was quick to action and disarmed her. I watched my father and Ivan drag her off the property.

I became aware of my children clinging to me. Their hiccupped sobs jolted my heart. I pulled them into my arms and whispered calming words. In a daze, I gathered Mitch into one arm and placed my hand on Kathy's shoulder to lead them to bed. I lay beside them and waited until they breathed calmly in their sleep. My mind was still in turmoil. It was apparent that we were dealing with an insane woman!

While Dad and Ivan were preoccupied with dispensing my nemesis, I phoned a trusted friend. I gave her a brief run-down on the reason we were leaving. She sighed. 'Ah, Aminia, I will be sad to see you go. And that Jan is an evil woman. She is very dangerous. She brags about the number of white men she has seduced. She says she has notches on her belt to remind her. Do you know she even slashed her mother's hands because she would not do what Jan wanted her to do? Although I will miss you, I'd rather know you and your children will be safe. Go in peace, my friend.'

As I hung up the phone, I heard my father's angry words, 'Ivan, you don't deserve my daughter. She has always supported you. You have dragged her from one school to another. It's about time you realised her value. You are a sorry excuse for a husband and father.'

Waking to a Nightmare
Deceived by a Charming, Narcissist Paedophile

Thankfully, nothing else happened that night. Although I was anxious, the moment I lay my head on my pillow, I was "out like a light",' as the saying goes. I didn't hear Ivan and Dad leave early that morning. Ivan had arranged a meeting with the outgoing principal of his new school. Dad went with him to help set up the house before Mum and I arrived with the children.

The sound of the removalist truck woke me at six a.m. I bounced out of bed, threw on my clothes, woke the children, prepared sandwiches, fruit, and drinks, and settled them into their car seats. I briefly spoke with the removalist. After one last look over the house we were leaving, I settled into the driver's seat; as I turned the car onto the road, I gave a deep sigh of relief, and tears again stung my eyes.

Dad had appraised Mum of the situation and informed her I would pick her up on my way. My mother tried to soothe my pain and hers, 'Never mind darling, all will be well. Ivan has had a scare, too, and I'm positive he will change his ways

Waking to a Nightmare
Deceived by a Charming, Narcissist Paedophile

now.' I'm sure Ivan used his Narcissistic charms to hoodwink my mother into believing he was a caring and wonderful husband who had made this one mistake.

It was clear how he wooed her. Each school holiday, we would go to my parent's home on the coast to spend time with the children at the beach or hiking in the bushland nearby. Ivan often ignored the children and me and preferred playing cards or doing crossword puzzles with my mother. But this episode exposed his flaws and rocked her assessment of him.

"You make your bed, you lie in it", still held me in its vice.

THE NARCISSIST WAS VISIBLY SHAKEN, AND HIS ARMOUR WAS CHINKED. HOW WAS HE TO REGAIN HIS POWER?

Waking to a Nightmare
Deceived by a Charming, Narcissist Paedophile

CHAPTER 9

It is incredible how news travels. A few months after arriving at our new home, I received a call from the principal who had replaced Ivan. 'Aminia, you were lucky to have escaped Jan. I've been warned to stay away from her. My mate, the Aboriginal Liaison Officer you met during your meeting with the "bigwigs", told me there was a full report on Jan's behaviour. It documents several of her violent and dangerous attacks. Ivan was not the only teacher she had an affair with either. The department has many reports about her assaults against other school members and some of the people in her community.'

How could these suits in The Department of Education not warn us of this woman's dangerous antics? One or more of these men would have signed off on the agreement that put Jan under my guidance for setting up the preschool. Indeed, this was negligence. What were they thinking?

Waking to a Nightmare
Deceived by a Charming, Narcissist Paedophile

Through the grapevine, we were later informed that Jan stabbed a new principal in the school due to some misunderstanding! My husband could pick them, eh?

As agreed during our meeting with the representatives of the Department of Education, we moved to the new school on the far south coast of NSW. Things, it seemed, were settling down. Ivan pulled me into his arms and whispered, 'Please, Aminia, can you forgive me? I know I can be a better husband. Let's put this all behind us and move on. I have learnt my lesson. From now on, I promise to make you and the children my priority.' I squeezed my eyes shut, trying to stem the hot tears that threatened to spill out. All I could do was nod. Ivan kissed me on the cheek and left. I staggered onto a chair and hugged myself. I wanted to believe his words, but he had repeatedly broken his promises.

Nowadays, a woman gets support from others if they go through what I experienced. However, those were different times. Even though I was doubtful Ivan would ever change,

Waking to a Nightmare
Deceived by a Charming, Narcissist Paedophile

I knew I wouldn't have any money or support if I left him. So, I had no choice. I decided to be more positive with the most heartfelt intention of sustaining our marriage, not for my sake but for my children.

It was a blessing that I had no clue what Ivan may have been doing at this new school. It was a time of personal healing for me.

A few months later, Ivan informed me that he had to attend an in-service course in Sydney at the start of the Christmas school holidays. We broke the long trip north by staying with his parents, who lived close to where Ivan was to attend his course. At the time, my parents were also in Sydney visiting friends. They agreed to pick me and the kids up and take us to their place on the far north coast. The children loved going there because the beach was nearby.

The day before Ivan was to leave to go to his seminar, he spent hours cleaning my car. I'm sure he liked to use my Alpha Romeo to impress the women. His mother

Waking to a Nightmare
Deceived by a Charming, Narcissist Paedophile

commented, 'Aminia, have you noticed that Ivan cleared everything out of your car, which suggests he has children?' My stomach flipped, and I knew there was truth in what she observed. Without a doubt, I knew he was up to his old philandering ways.

Ivan was supposed to be in Sydney for four days and planned to join us at my parents' house at the end of the week. The time for his arrival came and went. Strange as it may seem, I worried he might have had an accident. Mobile phones were not invented then. I phoned his mother. She didn't seem too concerned when I told her of my worry. 'He is probably studying with friends. He will turn up soon.' Her non-concern caused cold shivers to consume my body. Did she know something?

Three days late, Ivan pulled into my parents' driveway. I bolted downstairs. He was pulling his bags out of the car. 'Where have you been?' I demanded. He shrugged and

Waking to a Nightmare
Deceived by a Charming, Narcissist Paedophile

walked straight past me. I followed him into the room in which we were to sleep. 'Ivan, you are three days late!'

I watched him pull clothes from his bag. With a sneer, he half turned to me and said, 'Come on, Aminia, stop overreacting.'

'Overreacting! Are you crazy? I was worried sick, and the children kept asking why you did not come.'

'I met up with an old friend, and her family invited me to stay with them.' My innards turned to ice. I knew he had met with Jan. I accused him of doing so. He grabbed my arm and flung me around the room. Then he pushed me up against a set of drawers. I was petrified. He had never been violent like this before. 'Don't you ever accuse me of something you know nothing about!' Ivan was so close I felt his hot breath on my face. Then he sighed, pulled me into his arms, and said, 'Aminia, it's your fault. You make me so mad when you don't trust me.'

Waking to a Nightmare
Deceived by a Charming, Narcissist Paedophile

I pulled away from him and persisted, 'How hard would it have been for you to let me know you were okay? I was worried something might have happened to you.'

He grabbed my face, dug his fingers into my cheeks, and hissed. 'Well, if I want to visit Jan and her family, that is what I will do, and don't you ever question me again.' He let me go when we heard the children laughing as they bolted up the stairs. My parents had taken them to the beach. Ivan smiled and acted as though nothing had happened. And so did I.

'A LEOPARD NEVER CHANGES ITS SPOTS.' THE NARCISSIST WAS OUT OF CONTROL

Waking to a Nightmare
Deceived by a Charming, Narcissist Paedophile

CHAPTER 10

Ivan only had temporary tenure at the school on the South Coast, and when that time was up, he was sent to a school in the northwest of NSW.

I was working in the school residence...our new home...when a young man knocked on the door. 'Hi, I'm the new Social Science Teacher.' I invited him in and offered him a cuppa. His name was Darren. We hit it off immediately. We had a special connection, and our friendship grew.

A few months after Darren's arrival, a raging storm hit during the night. After Ivan and the children had left for school, I answered a knock on my door. A sad, soaking wet, mud-spattered Darren shivered on my doorstep. His flat was across the road from a hill with a piggery at the top. The downpour from the rain caused thick, muddy water to flow down and through his flat. His words came in static bursts, 'I

Waking to a Nightmare
Deceived by a Charming, Narcissist Paedophile

woke to a roaring sound and reached over the bed where I had my books. They were under smelly muddy water…ruined!' With a valiant effort, he choked back tears.

'Where are your clothes and shoes? I asked as I pulled him through my door.

He stared at me and hesitated before answering, 'Buried in thick mud along with all my reference books.'

'Have a shower, and I will find you some of Ivan's clothes you can wear.' While he showered, I cooked him breakfast.

Darren needed a place to live. My friend Maree said he could live in the cabin on her property until he found somewhere else. But Ivan had other plans. He told Darren to move into the room that adjoined our bedroom via two swinging doors. I raised my concerns with Ivan about the inappropriateness of this arrangement. My protests fell on deaf ears.

Not long after Darren moved in, I had an extreme reaction to some medication that my doctor prescribed. The district

Waking to a Nightmare
Deceived by a Charming, Narcissist Paedophile

nurse, Pat, saw the rash on my body and said in a worried voice, 'Aminia, you need to get to the hospital right now! I will drive you there!' The nearest hospital was 80 km away.

As soon as the doctor examined me, he gave me an injection and promptly admitted me to the hospital. I spent the night with two nurses applying thick calamine lotion over my body. At the time of my discharge, I was surprised when Darren arrived to take me home. I shook my head and mumbled, 'Where is Ivan?'

Darren's face flushed red, and he avoided looking at me. He settled me into his car and slammed the door. When he got behind the wheel, I asked, 'Darren, what is wrong with you?'

'That bastard of a husband of yours left this morning with the new teacher, Abby. He told me to take time off to go and fetch you from the hospital.'

Waking to a Nightmare
Deceived by a Charming, Narcissist Paedophile

I hung my head and stuttered, 'I…I'm sorry, Darren. If I'd known, I would have asked Maree or someone else to pick me up.'

Darren pulled over to the side of the road, stopped, and gathered me into his arms. 'Aminia, I don't mind picking you up. I'm not upset about that. I'm furious with your idiot husband. Pat told me how serious your condition was, and surely the doctor told Ivan that when he dropped you off at the hospital. What husband leaves his sick wife and goes off with another woman to a conference 280 km away?'

Ivan was up to his old lecherous ways, and Abby was fair prey. This was her first teaching post.

Darren settled me in back home and kept a close eye on me because the doctor had also informed him that if I had a further reaction, I would have to return to the hospital without delay.

Waking to a Nightmare
Deceived by a Charming, Narcissist Paedophile

On another occasion, Ivan and I took our children on an extended weekend stay at the lake, an hour's drive from our home. I was surprised when Darren told me that Ivan had invited him and Abby to join us. Abby couldn't come because her fiancé had arrived the night before. 'Fiancé! That was the first time we knew she had a Fiancé. When Darren conveyed this information, Ivan's eyes widened, and he stuttered some response before he sprinted into the bush. He didn't return for several hours and did not explain his behaviour.

Our family slept in our campervan, and Darren slept in the back of our station wagon. A little distance from our campsite was a fireplace where we cooked our meals. We gathered around the fire the first night, and one of Darren's mates joined us. He was staying in a tent a little further away. Amid much laughter and frivolity, we shared jokes and stories. Usually, Ivan would have been right into that. He sat

Waking to a Nightmare
Deceived by a Charming, Narcissist Paedophile

with his arms folded, staring into the fire, and remained mute.

Kathy and Mitch were curled up in their sleeping bags on a rug at our feet. Ivan stood up and said he was taking the children to bed. He did not return. Darren, his mate, and I stayed by the fire and told more yarns. I needed to go to the toilet, and my male companions walked me down the track to ensure there weren't snakes around. Darren's mate banged on the side of the toilet shed. I hauled up my pants and bolted out in surprise, bumped into Darren, and ended up on top of him on the ground. We giggled, and Darren helped me up. We headed back to the fire and noticed Ivan sitting there watching us.

I felt uncomfortable and went straight to bed in the campervan. A few minutes later, Ivan stood over me with his knuckles on his hips, 'Aminia, it is about time you went to bed with Darren.' I was distraught and cried into my pillow. Ivan hissed at me through clenched teeth, 'Be quiet; you will

Waking to a Nightmare
Deceived by a Charming, Narcissist Paedophile

wake the children. Go and sleep in the car with Darren.' Afraid he would hurt me again, I grabbed my sleeping bag, stumbled out the door and fell straight into Darren's arms. He had heard Ivan harassing me and was standing vigil.

He settled me on the front seat of the station wagon, slid beside me and cuddled me until my crying stopped. I melted into his embrace, feeling drained of all my energy. Darren lifted my chin, 'Aminia, you cannot go on like this. Come, you are distraught and exhausted. Let's climb into the back and sleep.' I woke with a start when I sensed someone watching us through the car's back window. I was right…it was Ivan! I bolted out of the car, into the campervan, and went to bed beside the children. Ivan did not return to the van. Where he slept, I did not know.

For most of the night, I tossed and turned. Darren was right about Ivan, but where would I go? I cried into my pillow until emotional exhaustion pulled me into a fitful sleep. When I woke, I was on my own. Ivan had risen early and

Waking to a Nightmare
Deceived by a Charming, Narcissist Paedophile

taken the children for a walk. I rolled over and buried my head into my pillow, trying to stifle more uncontrollable tears. Darren heard me weeping and peered through the van door. He gathered me in his arms, 'Oh Aminia, I hate seeing you like this…leave Ivan! He is a manipulative monster, and he will destroy you.' (prophetic words, in retrospect). But I knew it wasn't possible for me then. I was concerned that he would take my six-year-old Kathy, and I would never see her again.

I am sure Ivan was pushing Darren and me together so he would be free to have his affairs. I knew he would find a way to turn this whole sorry mess onto me and persuade others that I had betrayed him.

During the drive home, I was quiet and stared out the car window. Ivan also didn't speak. I jumped when his hands pounded the steering wheel, jolting me out of my thoughts. 'Aminia, you frustrate the hell out of me! I want you to have an affair with Darren.' I spun around and saw my children's four startled, frightened eyes peering at me.

I was speechless for a few minutes…I turned my angry, fire-filled eyes on him and snarled through clenched teeth, 'I will not do that because it would put Darren in a compromising position with you because you are his boss. And what's more, I do not want to involve Darren in our problems.' Ivan shrugged, then remained quiet for some time. He surprised me when he began laughing. 'You are such a prude, Aminia! You need to grow up!'

After that, I encouraged Darren to become a closer friend to Abby. This was impossible because Ivan spent most of his time with her. He manipulated his staff's work schedule so that she could accompany him when he went away on his frequent in-service trips. I now knew Ivan was back to his philandering behaviour. I am also sure his many trips did not involve educational matters.

Waking to a Nightmare
Deceived by a Charming, Narcissist Paedophile

As I entered the school office door the following day, Merril waved a piece of paper to attract my attention. 'I think you should apply for this. It is an application for a two-year tenure as a Community Arts Officer, and I know that would suit your artistic and community spirit perfectly.'

I read the document and filled it in, thinking other people would be more qualified than me, and I had little hope of getting the position. When I arrived at the interviewing venue, the waiting room was full of applicants. I was the last person called into the interviewing room. Five people sat on one side of a large oval table. They fired questions at me. When the interview was complete, I was told I would be informed if I had the job in a few days. I got it!

At first, the job was challenging. I visited many community groups to ascertain what they wanted to see developed in their community. I took extensive notes and recordings of their thoughts and, from these, developed appropriate procedures. I did weekly radio sessions and talked about

Waking to a Nightmare
Deceived by a Charming, Narcissist Paedophile

what the communities wanted and later were achieving, such as art exhibitions, playwriting, acting and much more. However, when I first spoke on the radio, I'm sure my nerves were apparent, but soon, these settled, and I looked forward to my weekly broadcasts. The artist in me encouraged schools to support their pupil's artistic talents by allowing them to do murals on their walls. This job was my true calling. I revelled in it.

I confided in Ivan about how I felt. He promised he would not apply for a position in another school until my tenure as the Community Arts Officer ended at the end of the following school year.

Things were coming to a head in the school because people expressed dissatisfaction with some of Ivan's activities in and out of school. He decided to apply for a promotion to teach in a larger school. That required him to write an extensive report documenting his improvements in this school and expand on the methods he would use to improve any future school where he would be the principal. Ivan was not putting in the time necessary to do this because he was still caught up in what I called *his extracurricular activities*—entertaining his young lady teacher.

His inspection regarding this promotion was to occur immediately after the winter break. Ivan had not put pen to paper and decided to pull out of the process. This was impossible because he had missed the date to cancel his Promotion Application. Ivan was frantic and even suggested he should resign.

Being the supportive wife, I came up with a plan. 'Calm down. We will send the children to their grandparents. That will free up some of my time so I can help you compile your report for the inspectors. However, I have one condition. You will not apply to move to another school position until I complete my work.' Ivan promised faithfully that he would abide by my request.

Waking to a Nightmare
Deceived by a Charming, Narcissist Paedophile

The help I gave Ivan was reminiscent of the days I did his assignments for university, and he did not doubt that I could deliver. After completing the document, which was quite extensive, I advised him to read it over several times to familiarise himself with its content. However, Ivan's ego was such that he only read it once. He informed me, 'Aminia, you worry too much. I know my job and will wrap rings around these inspectors.'

When the two inspectors arrived, Ivan was very nervous. The process took two long days. One of the inspectors spent some time in my room while I was teaching and afterwards asked me questions. Late on the second day, the elder of the two inspectors came into the room where I was teaching. 'Aminia, we are not going to give your husband the promotion. We can't work him out. He is an enigma to us. My colleague and I have tried to fathom who and what he is, and he remains a mystery. He presents as a charming person to us when working with the children. However, his staff are reluctant to say much about him. The most disturbing thing is that he fumbled many times when we questioned him about the document he submitted, which outlined his achievements here and why he deserved this promotion. On the other hand, you were a delight to meet, and we are impressed with what you have achieved in this and other schools in your role as the Community Arts Officer. Good luck, Aminia.'

After this, Ivan withdrew into himself. His love affair with Libby was not going well, and he became morose.

NARCISSISTS ARE LIARS AND ONLY LOOK AFTER THEIR INTERESTS.

Waking to a Nightmare
Deceived by a Charming, Narcissist Paedophile

CHAPTER 11

Things seemed to be settling for me, but the peace didn't last long. A severe mouse plague hit! The sound of my children's screams at night haunted me. Mice ran up the curtains and over their bodies…there was no respite from these creatures. Even writing about this sends chills down my spine!

It was becoming challenging to be in these conditions. If visitors from other schools or the Department visited, Ivan would ask me to provide them with a meal. Usually, I cooked on the fuel stove, but I also used the electric stove when cooking for more people.

On one such day, I turned the oven on. The unbearable smell drove me backwards, gagging. Dead mice were in the stove lining. The infernal stench of mouse droppings and the acrid smell of their urine filled the kitchen. I wrapped a wet cloth around my face and steeled myself to clean the mess. I could

Waking to a Nightmare
Deceived by a Charming, Narcissist Paedophile

only stay there for a few seconds before feeling nauseous and needing fresh air.

This was too much!

Only the week before, a representative from Teacher Housing informed me that our house was at the top of the list for renovations. Still feeling sickened by the situation, I rang Teacher Housing and enquired about the start date for the renovations. I was horrified when I was informed that our scheduled renovation had been moved from the top spot to the twentieth on the list.

I exploded, 'What! Are you serious? I can barely be in this house for a minute without feeling sick! My children can't sleep because these bloody pests wake them, and their screaming wakes Ivan and me. I cannot even use the stove. This house is a health hazard! Please transfer me to the person responsible for this list?'

Waking to a Nightmare
Deceived by a Charming, Narcissist Paedophile

My knuckles gleamed white as I held on tight to the phone. Then I heard the person on the other end talking to someone. Eventually, a male voice greeted me. Again, I explained the situation. He tried to soothe me, but I was not having a bar of it. 'If somebody is not out here by the end of the week to reassess this house, I will leave here, but that will not be the end. I will tell the papers and television reporters about your negligence in caring for your teachers and their family members.'

I was assured that a team would assess the situation the next day. That afternoon, I informed Ivan about this. His face reddened, and he backed me into a corner, 'How dare you talk to my superiors like that! Do you realise that may go against me?' The noise of the door slamming as our children darted through caused him to back away.

The men who inspected our house were appalled by the conditions in which my family lived. One of the men declared, 'We will expedite the process and fix all the problems as soon as possible. He also assured me that my house would be reinstated to the top of the list. I'm sure this would not have been the outcome if I hadn't been so insistent. When it came to the welfare of my children, I would not back down. I was sure my children's health was at risk. So again, the lioness stepped forward.

A team of draftsmen visited two days later. After inspecting the house, they recommended demolishing and replacing it with a demountable house. 'Are you kidding? I exclaimed. 'Those houses are extremely uncomfortable in the heat of summer and the cold of winter!' I asked them to wait while I retrieved my art book. In nearly every house I had lived in, I would draw plans for design improvements, and I had done so for this house. When I showed my plans to these men, they were impressed. We walked around the rooms as I explained my ideas. One of the men asked where I had learnt my skills. 'Redesigning to improve houses is a hobby of

Waking to a Nightmare
Deceived by a Charming, Narcissist Paedophile

mine. My father and I have renovated a few houses. And I also studied interior design in Uni.'

The boss man of the group smiled widely. 'Aminia, I believe you are right about this. It is doable and will make a much better house for family living, particularly considering this area's extreme summer heat and cold winters! Can we have a copy of your designs?' I handed him a copy I had already made. 'We will start on this house very soon.' This was music to my ears, and I did my famous Irish jig throughout the house.

A few weeks later, Ivan received a phone call from the people in charge of the house renovation. They said that they would start working on the house the following week. Ivan asked where we would be housed. The voice on the phone told him they would put us up in the motel in the nearest town, which was 80 kilometres away. Ivan, who would never buck the authority, agreed.

Waking to a Nightmare
Deceived by a Charming, Narcissist Paedophile

When he told me this news, I was alarmed. 'Ivan, are you serious? That's too much travel for Kathy and Mitch!'

I spoke to Maree about this, and she didn't hesitate to find the perfect solution. 'Why don't you stay at my house? A wing of the house has two bedrooms, a bathroom, and a kitchen.' Maree's home was originally an old homestead, and she and her husband had moved into town from one of the large sheep stations. 'I hugged her, and my body relaxed for the first time in days. When I told Ivan this excellent news, he shrugged and walked away.

That evening, he informed me, 'I have arranged our accommodation. Kathy can stay at Maree's, and Mitch will live at Bart's (his best schoolmate, who lived 30 kilometres away). He will love it there because he enjoys being at the sheep station. And I have arranged for us to stay in Darren's flat.'

I couldn't believe what I was hearing. 'Where in Darren's place will we be sleeping? It is only a two-bedroom unit, and the new infant's teacher has one bedroom, and Darren has the other.'

Ivan grinned and said, 'I have arranged everything. You and I will sleep in the loungeroom on a mattress.'

Something inside me snapped. I was disgusted because I knew Ivan was again scheming to push Darren and me together. I pursed my lips, trying not to explode, but to no avail…I exploded, 'Are you serious? Why are you doing this? I will not cope with being separated from my children! Maree gave us the perfect solution. Have you lost your mind?'

Ivan smirked, turned his back to me, and walked away. I knew he wouldn't listen to reason. He had other plans.

HE WAS THE ULTIMATE NARCISSIST AFTER ALL.

I was like a zombie and was often tearful. One night, I overheard Darren arguing with Ivan about how hard it was for me to be separated from my children. Not to mention, I had little sleep due to the uncomfortable situation.

A week later, Ivan announced that we were going on holiday. 'I have accrued a month's service leave, which will take us up to the Christmas School Holidays, giving us two months to enjoy.'

The crew working on the house had to stop at various times because they had difficulty getting the needed materials and because it was impossible to work in the extreme summer heat.

Ivan was very clever at torturing me and then reeling me back in. I must admit I thoroughly enjoyed the holiday, and for some reason, Ivan seemed different. He played more with the children and seemed to enjoy my company. This time was reminiscent of the days of our courting. But I questioned his motives now and wondered how long this would last. I could never relax…

Waking to a Nightmare
Deceived by a Charming, Narcissist Paedophile

THIS NARCISSIST, SPIDER, WAS PLAYING WITH ITS VICTIM.

Waking to a Nightmare
Deceived by a Charming, Narcissist Paedophile

CHAPTER 12

The house that I had been so excited to move into, the same place that was being renovated using my designs… we never got to occupy…how sad I felt is beyond words!

What happened is the pure work of THE NARCISSIST.

One day after the close of school, I was walking past the office when I heard the phone ringing. I rushed to answer it. After the male voice on the phone verified who I was, he informed me that the school transfer Ivan had applied for on the hinterland of the north coast of NSW was available for him to inspect. I was flabbergasted and questioned him about who had put in for this transfer. The voice assured me it was Ivan. I had no clue about it. Ivan knew I still had one more year to complete my tenure as The Community Arts Officer. He had promised me he wouldn't apply for another move until that time ended. I sat on the top step of the school verandah, and silent tears rolled down my cheeks. Why had

Waking to a Nightmare
Deceived by a Charming, Narcissist Paedophile

Ivan applied for this move without any discussion with me? How easy it was for him to break his promises. My needs were never a concern.

I felt my trust had been violated yet again! I bounced up and sprinted to find Ivan, who was in Darren's flat. As I entered the door, I screamed through my sobs, 'Ivan, why did you apply for a move when you promised we would not move until my tenure as the Community Arts Officer ended?'

Ivan stood over me and backed me against the wall. 'Come on, Aminia; calm down.'

My words exploded in static sobs, 'But you promised me we would not move until I had finished my work! You went behind my back and made this decision.' I didn't realise until he grasped my hands that I was pounding his chest.

Ivan held my wrists and pulled me in tight. 'Listen to me. This will be a great move for all of us. We can visit your parents often as the school is only forty minutes away. Just

Waking to a Nightmare
Deceived by a Charming, Narcissist Paedophile

come with me and have a look. Then, if you don't like the idea, we will discuss it afterwards.'

The Department of Education had granted him three days of paid leave to inspect the school. We left just after lunch that day, a Thursday, giving us four days to check out the new school and spend time with my parents. Our children stayed at their friend's place.

Ivan's nephew, Gerry, had come to visit at this time and was staying on a farm not far from us. Ivan asked his brother to meet us along the way to take his son home. When I went to get into the car, I was surprised to find Gerry was occupying the front seat. I was even more surprised when I noticed Darren sitting in the back seat. He had the flu and had three days of sick leave left. I asked Gerry to sit in the back with Darren, but Ivan told him to stay where he was. Once again, Ivan manipulated the situation to ensure Darren and I were pushed together! What could have been an enjoyable road

Waking to a Nightmare
Deceived by a Charming, Narcissist Paedophile

trip became a nightmare. Darren and I often caught Ivan's beady eyes staring at us through the rearview mirror!

We drove through the night… it was a nine-and-a-half-hour trip. I took the wheel for a period, and Ivan sat in the back with his nephew, forcing Darren to sit in front with me. There were still a further three hours to go, so we stopped to get some food and freshen up. Again, Ivan drove with Gerry in the front. Darren and I were relegated to the rear seat again. Darren gently pulled my head onto his lap and said, 'Come on, let's get some shuteye,'

I woke when Ivan pulled the car into a service station where Gerry's father met us. Ivan sat in the front alone for the rest of the trip. We arrived at my parents' house at midnight. After exchanging greetings, we went to bed. I woke early the following day and headed down to the beach for a dip. Darren saw me leave the house and followed me. We had a great time catching the waves.

Waking to a Nightmare
Deceived by a Charming, Narcissist Paedophile

After breakfast, we all (including my parents) headed to the new school, about an hour's trip down the coast.

After visiting the school, I told Ivan I would not be happy for our children to attend. 'They have moved around since they were toddlers. They are happy in the school where we live now. It's the first time they have been able to make close friends. It would be traumatic for them to be uprooted again. And you promised we would not move until I completed my Community Arts Officer tenure. You know how much time and effort I have put into setting it up, and I am enjoying what I do. Please, Ivan, you promised me the next move was my choice.'

But none of this mattered to Ivan. He had already decided, and my opinion was worthless to him. He accepted the position without any further discussion. He suggested I move into Maree's house so I could continue my job and the children could stay with me.

Waking to a Nightmare
Deceived by a Charming, Narcissist Paedophile

When this was suggested to Kathy, she burst into sobs and ran from the house. When she returned later, she hissed at me, 'It's all your fault! 'Why do we have to move?' And if Dad moves, I'm going with him, and you and Mitch can stay here!'

I could not contemplate being separated from Kathy, so I resigned from my job and agreed to shift on the condition that we buy and live in a house in the nearest town, and the children would attend school there.

As I look back on my life with this NARCISSIST, I'm sure he took great pleasure in clipping my wings. Was he jealous of me? Maybe. Was he Controlling? That gets a resounding YES!

I wasn't always the compliant wife. On three separate occasions, I tried to leave him. The first instance happened when Kathy was five, and Mitch was three. I packed the car, buckled the kids into their seats, and drove up the road, but the road was closed off, and the way around was too far.

Waking to a Nightmare
Deceived by a Charming, Narcissist Paedophile

Letting out a frustrated growl, I turned around. As I drove home, I lamented how the universe conspired against me.

The second time, I packed the kids into my car and headed to my parent's place. Dad was away playing in a golf tournament. With a lump in my throat and tears brimming, ready to fall, I told Mum some of my story. Mum hugged me while I sobbed. Then she held me at arm's length and said, 'Aminia, you will have to go back to Ivan and find a way to make your marriage work.' Although she didn't say, YOU MAKE YOUR BED YOU LIE IN IT, those words rang in my mind.

On the third occasion, I was packing my car to leave. Darren was teaching in the room that looked out to our driveway. He sensed something was wrong with me (he was always very empathetic towards me; he was a good friend). As I put the last item in the car, he appeared beside me and said, 'Where do you think you are going?'

Waking to a Nightmare
Deceived by a Charming, Narcissist Paedophile

I turned away from him and forced my words to leave my choked throat, 'I'm leaving. I can't live with Ivan anymore. He is evil.'

Darren held me tight and whispered, 'Well, I'm not going to let you leave alone; I'm going too. I'll pack and then get your kids out of class. You go inside and pack their gear.'

I pulled free, 'No!' I cried, 'You can't do that. It will be the end of your career!'

'I don't care about my career. I care more about you. It breaks my heart when I see how that excuse for a husband of yours treats you.'

I had no other choice. I wasn't going to let Darren end his career. I unpacked the car and stayed. Emotionally, I felt like a pinata being attacked from all sides by Ivan.

A couple of nights on, I was woken by Abby's giggling. Was I mistaken? Was I dreaming? I heard her giggle again. She and Ivan sat on the verandah steps, a metre from my

Waking to a Nightmare
Deceived by a Charming, Narcissist Paedophile

bedroom. I quietly went to the window and peeked out. They were cuddling, and I thought he was tickling her. I suspected they must have heard me because Ivan suddenly stood up, and Abby scooted off.

Abby and I went on a school in-service course together, and she made a rather strange comment, 'I don't know why you and Darren don't get together. It is obvious how he feels about you.'

I sat quietly, contemplating what she had said. 'Yes, I did love Darren, and I know he loved me, but I would never have a sexual relationship with him because my husband was his boss and had the power to terminate Darren's career. By now, I knew Ivan's warped character. I was sure Ivan would delight in using his position to hurt Darren and me. The Narcissist must always have the upper hand. Although it pained me, I know it was the right decision because now Darren has an important teaching position.'

Waking to a Nightmare
Deceived by a Charming, Narcissist Paedophile

Not long after Ivan started working at his new school, we purchased a lovely house in the nearest town, and the children went to school there. I enrolled in university, and later in the year, while I was away on a field trip, Ivan suffered a burst appendix. As I turned the car into our driveway, I was met by a stormy-faced Mother-in-law. I hadn't even managed to get out of my car when she pulled my door open, and she accosted me with her belligerent voice, 'Well, I hope you enjoyed your holiday while my son was in the hospital fighting for his life!'

I questioned why no one contacted me. Mind you, there were no mobile phones back then. However, we students left our home contact details with the park ranger where we were, and I left my contact details on our noticeboard for Ivan.

Kathy and Mitch overheard their grandmother talking about how sick their father was and that he could die. Kathy asked me if she could phone Darren. I overheard her say, 'Darren, our Daddy is dying. Will you come and be our Daddy?'

Waking to a Nightmare
Deceived by a Charming, Narcissist Paedophile

I knew Darren was fond of my children, and they loved him. When Kathy and Mitch finished their conversation, I took the phone and asked Darren what he had replied. His answer startled me…'I told them, yes, I would love to be your daddy.'

For a moment, I was speechless. Then, in a hesitant whisper, I said, 'Darren, you shouldn't have said that.'

'Why not, Aminia? You must know how much I love you and your children.'

His love for me was evident in something he said to me once, 'If I can't have you, then I will find someone just like you.' He did, and I believe they have a successful marriage.

Waking to a Nightmare
Deceived by a Charming, Narcissist Paedophile

CHAPTER 13

Why did I not leave this NARCISSIST? Why was he so intent on keeping me from living the life I craved? One of being loved and supported in my endeavours and dreams. It seemed Ivan was intent on ensuring my desires never came to fruition. Why? I could not understand. I fully supported him in all his activities. Despite my suffering, I pulled myself up and somehow found it in me to carry on. My kids became the reason for my survival. And along the way, I came across people who became part of my support system.

The only shining light in our next move was the new house Ivan and I bought. It was beautiful and looked out over rolling hills from our back verandah. On Kathy's first day at her new school, she met Alice, who lived around the corner from our new address. Alice also had a young brother, and he and Mitch explored the area together on their bikes. Alice's parents became our friends, and we shared good

Waking to a Nightmare
Deceived by a Charming, Narcissist Paedophile

times filled with laughter, food, drinks, and occasional outings.

About twelve months on, Ivan and I were in his office when he received a phone call. I overheard the person on the phone yelling hysterically. Ivan froze, and his face turned scarlet. Sheer terror masked his mottled red face. Ivan thrust the phone into my hand and slumped back in his chair, his face drained of colour. I was shocked and confused. After a minute's hesitation, I spoke to the person on the phone. 'Please calm down and tell me why you are upset.'

It took the caller a few seconds before he stopped shouting. Through his sobbing, he tried to convey his garbled message. I couldn't understand what he was saying until he drew a long breath and, with venom in every word, exclaimed, 'Why can't you keep your husband satisfied? Now, he is splitting up my marriage and taking my wife and daughter away from me!' With a loud click, the phone call ended.

Waking to a Nightmare
Deceived by a Charming, Narcissist Paedophile

I felt sick, my jaws clenched tight, and my knees threatened to give way. I backed up to a chair and flopped in it. What was going on? I gulped in a few deep breaths to calm myself. 'What the hell was that all about, Ivan?'

Ivan clasped the sides of his head and shook, 'Dammed if I know! I think he's lost his mind and is talking crazy. I haven't a clue what's got into him.' Ivan stood, pulled himself out of his chair, and stumbled to me. He wrapped me in a tight hug. 'You know, Aminia, you're my only '. I have changed! I am not the silly person I was anymore! Please believe me. Don't listen to the rantings of that crazy man. His wife warned me about his heavy drinking and how he has been accusing her of things she is not doing. Come. Let's go home and put this behind us.'

When we arrived home, Ivan was unusually attentive. He poured me a wine and cooked dinner while I relaxed. Once again, the talented Narcissist manipulated me. And again, I fell right into his trap.

Waking to a Nightmare
Deceived by a Charming, Narcissist Paedophile

The next day was a Saturday, and I was doing my housework while Ivan was planting in our vegetable patch. I was busy vacuuming when the phone rang. I turned off the machine and rushed to pick up the call. It was Rhonda, Alice's mother, the wife of Ivan's distraught accuser of the day before.

'Where is Ivan?' she demanded.

Although I was taken aback, I quickly recovered and said, 'He is out in the garden. Why?'

'No, you are lying. He is meeting me in Gosford today!' This town was 130 km away.

'Well, he certainly isn't in Gosford. He is here.'

She exploded. 'You're lying. I spoke to him late last night, and he told me he was all packed and would leave early this morning.' I slammed the phone into its hook.

My mind was reeling. What the hell was going on? My legs became jelly as I exited the house and confronted Ivan. 'What is going on with you and Rhonda?'

Waking to a Nightmare
Deceived by a Charming, Narcissist Paedophile

Ivan raised his head and then pushed himself up, 'What do you mean? What are you babbling on about this time, Aminia?'

'She says you were supposed to meet her in Gosford today. Is that true?'

Ivan wiped the sweat from his brow and sneered at me, 'Aminia, you are as big a nutcase as Rhonda and her husband are if you believe that. She wanted me to leave you and meet her, but I told her she was crazy, and it seemed I was right. And if you believe her and her husband, you have also lost the plot. I have not promised her anything, and I haven't any intention of leaving you! But if you keep doubting me, maybe I should!'

Thank goodness Kathy and Mitch were not home at the time. Mitch was off riding his bike with a couple of his schoolmates, and Kathy was away playing hockey with her team. How would I tell Kathy that her best friend had left and was not returning?

Waking to a Nightmare
Deceived by a Charming, Narcissist Paedophile

Kathy's reaction hit me like a blow to my stomach. She screamed, 'No, you're lying! They were supposed to wait until Dad could take me and them with him!'

I almost fainted and plopped into a chair. I knew she would react strongly to this news, but what she said was unbelievable. She continued, 'Mum, it's like this: Dad doesn't love you and Mitch. He loves me. We are leaving. Dad says he and I will live with Rhonda and Alice!' Kathy bolted into her room and slammed the door.

I slid to the floor with my back to Kathy's door. My sobbing racked through every fibre of my body until I had no more tears. I pulled myself up and, like a person in a dream, walked to my wardrobe, pulled a suitcase down, and frantically threw clothes and a few more essentials into it. Then I gathered the kid's clothes from the washing basket. I packed the car and strapped Mitch in his seat. Kathy heard me and ran to me, 'Where are you going, Mum?'

Waking to a Nightmare
Deceived by a Charming, Narcissist Paedophile

'Jump in your seat. We are going away for a while to Nan and Pop's for a beach holiday.'

She ran to the car's other side, jumped in, and clipped her seatbelt. Ivan came to the car door. With frantic fingers, I locked the doors. His muffled voice asked me where I was going. 'I need time away from you to work out what I want to do.'

'Please don't go. Come inside and talk about this. I'm sure we can work it out together.' I turned the key and planted my foot on the accelerator. I didn't even care if I ran over his foot. This time, he would not win me over with his clever words. His hung head was the vision of him through my rearview mirror. The Narcissist had not gotten what he wanted.

Kathy watched her father slump. 'Mum, go back and get Dad. He is crying.' I drew a steading breath to settle myself and explained, 'Daddy can't join us because he has to work, and that is why he is sad.'

Waking to a Nightmare
Deceived by a Charming, Narcissist Paedophile

As I turned off my car at my parents' house, Mum and Dad appeared at my door. Stepping out of the car, I found myself wrapped in their arms. I was shocked by this reception. Mum guided me up the stairs after giving Dad instructions to take care of the kids. I was ushered into her bedroom, and she closed the door behind us. 'What on Earth is going on with you and Ivan? He rang, all upset because you left him. I want to know why.' My gushing tears choked me, and I could not get any words out.

Mum handed me a wad of tissues and told me to settle down. After gulping in a few deep breaths, I was able to speak. 'I'm leaving him.'

Mum's lips were tight as she held me at arm's length and demanded, 'Aminia, why?'

I told her what had happened. She drew a long breath and said, 'But Ivan is distraught. He told me one of the parents of a child he taught was out to get him for some reason and had twisted your mind against him. You must go back and sort this out. He says you haven't been well and have been confused about many things lately. You have been saying crazy things and accusing him of misbehaving with other women. He is adamant that you are mistaken and wants you to get some help to sort out your mind.'

AGAIN, THE NARCISSIST MANIPULATED THE SITUATION SO THAT I WAS THE PROBLEM.

Waking to a Nightmare
Deceived by a Charming, Narcissist Paedophile

CHAPTER 14

As my marital life became increasingly unbearable, other issues regarding Ivan's Duty of Care for his students were about to be revealed that severely impacted our relationship.

Ivan persuaded a lady home-schooling her son and her foster daughter, Inka, to enrol the children in his school. She agreed and persuaded her friend to enrol her son, too. These three children and some tweaking of the number of students, some having left the school, made it possible to retain the school's present number of teachers.

At the start of the Easter School Holidays, Ivan received a phone call from Kate, the mother of two young boys who attended his school. I overheard this troubled woman's raised voice, 'I am very concerned about an issue regarding my two sons! That girl, Inka, you insisted should be enrolled in the school, even though the representatives of the Department of Child Welfare advised you not to, has been

Waking to a Nightmare
Deceived by a Charming, Narcissist Paedophile

enticing my boys and another boy into the all-weather shed and has been performing sexual acts with them. She is twelve, and my boys are only five and six! I want you to come to my place and discuss this today!'

Ivan attempted to replace the phone on its cradle, but his hands shook so much that it clattered onto the bench. His face revealed pure fear when he turned to me. His meek request for me to accompany him while he spoke with this lady surprised me. Although I was also shocked by the extent of the anger I overheard in the mother's voice, my heart was with her in this matter.

During the 40-minute drive to the lady's home, Ivan devised his strategy to placate or silence this concerned mother. He decided to visit the mother of the other boy first. Both parents were home. They told us that Kate had contacted them and had informed them about what had happened to her boys and their son. Ivan persuaded them not to make a

Waking to a Nightmare
Deceived by a Charming, Narcissist Paedophile

big deal of it or even report it because it would harm their son, who had a behavioural and learning disability.

He also played the situation down, saying the other woman overreacted and would cause more harm than good. The complaining family was new to the district, while this family had known Ivan for a long time, liked him, and, therefore, took his advice.

Feeling satisfied with the outcome of this meeting, Ivan visited Pam, the mother, who had reported the incident. Her husband, Barry, was present and was furious about what had happened to his sons. He pranced around the room, waving his hands and shouting. Then he grabbed Ivan by his shirt and pulled his face close to his, 'What sort of a Headmaster are you? Where was your duty of care? It is your job to ensure all the children in your school are safe.' What will you do to make sure this does not happen again?'

Ivan pulled out all his charm, convincing them that he was empathetic to their concerns for their children and would do

Waking to a Nightmare
Deceived by a Charming, Narcissist Paedophile

all he could to ensure this situation would never arise again. Although the parents were still upset, Ivan assured them that he would meet with his staff and instruct them to be more diligent in supervising all the children in the school. I will also tell the girl's foster mother to come and watch her during recess and lunch breaks.

Pam warned him, 'I will hold you fully responsible should this happen again. And I assure you I will not hesitate to take the matter further.'

During our drive home, Ivan was chuffed with the outcome and bragged to me, 'No doubt about it, I have great skills when it comes to handling irate parents.'

I sat staring out of the car window, feeling sick. This excuse for a school principal and a father did not deserve to hold a position of caring for children.

Waking to a Nightmare
Deceived by a Charming, Narcissist Paedophile

Another disturbing incident happened early the following year. The children were travelling by bus to the Small School District Swimming Carnival.

Ivan and his new flame, Sharlet, sat in front of the bus with another teacher, exchanging jokes with the bus driver. They did not notice what was happening between Inka and Connor at the back of the bus.

The next day, I was shopping in town, and Pam approached and asked me to have a coffee with her. As I sipped my drink, she relayed this horrifying incident to me. 'I picked Conner up from school after the swimming carnival. He was quiet and ran to the car without greeting me. I watched him in my rearview mirror. He was hunched up in the back of the car and upset about something. I tried several times to engage him in conversation about how his day at the pool went, but he only responded with grunted replies. Later, when I tucked him into bed, he cried and spluttered, 'Mum, I'm sorry.'

I asked him, 'Sorry for what, Connor?'

Waking to a Nightmare
Deceived by a Charming, Narcissist Paedophile

My boy struggled to say, 'I'm sorry, Mum; I tried not to sit near Inka, but she pulled Erick out of the seat and sat down with me. Mum, Inka is scary. She said she would report me to the teachers for swearing if I didn't do what she wanted.'

I asked, 'What did she ask you to do, Connor?'

What Pam said next shocked me.

'These are my son's words etched into my mind, she said as her voice hitched. 'I'm sorry, Mum. She made me put that yellow suncream stuff inside her between her legs. I tried to get past her, but she is bigger than me, and I couldn't.'

'Aminia, he was so upset he kept sobbing and repeating, ' I'm sorry, Mum. I did it.'

I reached over the table, placed my hand over Pam's, and uttered, 'I'm so sorry your son suffered that. No wonder you are angry. What do you intend to do about this?'

'Judging by your reaction, Aminia, I can tell you are sympathetic towards me and concerned about the boys. It

Waking to a Nightmare
Deceived by a Charming, Narcissist Paedophile

must be hard for you to be married to that terrible man. My husband is off work tomorrow, and we intend to confront Ivan about this.'

The following day, I was compiling the articles to be included in the School and Community Newspaper in the room adjoining Ivan's office when I heard Connor's irate parents yelling. They demanded that Inka be removed from the school. Ivan stood his ground and said, 'You cannot demand me to do that. Anyway, what is all this commotion about? I think you two are just out to make trouble.'

Connor's father, Barry, exploded, 'Trouble! I'll give you trouble! You promised us you would make sure she stayed away from our boys. Instead, you, your girlfriend, and that other teacher sat in front of the bus and paid no attention to what was happening with the children.'

I cracked the door between Ivan's office and the printing room and peeped in. Pam reached over and placed a soothing hand on her husband's arm, and he stopped abusing Ivan.

Waking to a Nightmare
Deceived by a Charming, Narcissist Paedophile

With a quiet determination in her voice, Pam, the President of the School's Parents and Citizen's Association, calmly announced, 'Now this is what will happen. I contacted all the members of the Parents and Citizens Association last night and called an urgent public meeting for tomorrow. I have also contacted the school authorities and a Child Welfare representative. Barry and I will relay what happened to our sons and insist this troublesome girl be removed from this school. In my opinion, it seems you and your staff are unable, or even worse, unwilling to protect our children from her promiscuous behaviour. So, you leave us with no choice but to take matters into our own hands.'

Two hours before the set time for the Parents and Citizens' meeting, Ivan met with two dignitaries from the Department of Education and a Department of Community Services representative.

Earlier, Ivan instructed me to take all the children into the library before the meeting began. I knew he did not want me

Waking to a Nightmare
Deceived by a Charming, Narcissist Paedophile

to attend because he suspected I would speak the truth and take the side of the offended parents, and that is precisely what I would have done.

As the clock on the wall chimed for 10 o'clock, the parents assembled, and a little after, Ivan and the men in suits emerged from his office. Without delay, I ushered the children into the library and closed the door.

About an hour later, Ivan burst through the library door, dismissed the children, and declared, 'I won!'

'What do you mean you won?' I asked.

'Well, the representatives of the Department of Education knew that if we didn't put a stop to the accusations of those troublemakers, their heads, along with mine, would probably roll!' Ivan pranced around the room and clapped his hands. The smirk on his face widened, 'I knew exactly what to do. I told them things that made it obvious Pam and Barry were lying. So yes, it's a bloody good win! And Sharlet backed me up by declaring there was no yellow zinc cream on Inka's clothing.' So, it was obvious the boy had made it up. But what's even better is that Pam and Barry have been told that their boys will be removed from the school, and Pam must resign as president of the P & C.'

I was dumbfounded, and tears filled my eyes as I thought of those little boys having to leave their friends and travel on the high school student's bus at 7 a.m. each morning and not arrive home in the afternoon until after 5 p.m.

My anger exploded, 'How can that be the outcome? What is wrong with you men? Those little boys are innocent, and their parents are only trying to protect them. You and your buddies disgust me. You treat it like a game you and your cronies had to win! All of you are only interested in protecting your precious jobs. But what about the protection of the children? None of you deserve to hold the positions you do!'

Waking to a Nightmare
Deceived by a Charming, Narcissist Paedophile

That afternoon, Ivan took Kathy to her hockey practice. I was surprised when Sharlet visited me on the farm. She asked me to take a walk with her while she collected firewood. Although I was reluctant to be in her company, something led me to join her. The subject of Connor smearing yellow zinc cream into Inka's vagina arose. With a wicked grin, Sharlet said, 'You know, Aminia. It was great that we won over those people. Ivan would have lost his job if I hadn't lied and told the people at the meeting that Inka did not have any yellow stains on her panties.'

I stopped dead in my tracks and confronted this despicable woman. 'You lied? How could you gloat over what you did to those poor little boys and their parents? You are evil!'

Sharlet looked me in the eye and smirked, 'Well, it's simple: I didn't want Ivan to lose his job.'

'Did Ivan know about this?'

Waking to a Nightmare
Deceived by a Charming, Narcissist Paedophile

'Of course. Ivan and I discussed what I would say at the meeting to make out that Connor's parents made everything up because they didn't like Ivan and wanted him removed from the school.'

I threw down the firewood I had collected, 'You and Ivan disgust me! You deserve each other! Then, as fast as possible, I strode away from this despicable person.

THE NARCISSIST HAD HIS PERFECT MATCH.

Waking to a Nightmare
Deceived by a Charming, Narcissist Paedophile

CHAPTER 15

When Ivan arrived home, he was furious. 'How dare you question my actions? You have no standing in my school. You are nothing more than a casual teacher and office manager, and you will keep your comments to yourself. And you will show Sharlet the respect she deserves!'

A sinister smile twisted his features as he bragged, 'I am too smart for any of those parents to make an impact on my career. I won, and that is the end of the matter.'

Those two little boys of the complaintive family had to leave the school and go to another school, leaving their school friends behind. I was heartbroken for them. Drawing all my reserves, I again confronted Ivan. 'Please, Ivan, where is your compassion for these innocent children? It is your job to protect the welfare of all children in your care!'

Waking to a Nightmare
Deceived by a Charming, Narcissist Paedophile

Two days later, I was horrified when I heard some of the older children shouting abuse over the school fence at Barry. He jumped out of his car and ran through the school gate, yelling at the children. Ivan heard the commotion, sprang out of his office, and confronted him. Everyone could hear Barry abusing Ivan. 'You are a rotten example for these children. You know the truth, and you lied. I will not rest until the truth is told.'

I did not hear what Ivan said, but out of my window, I saw Barry leave through the school gate. When Ivan came back, he had a scrape on his chin and told me and the staff, who were on lunch break, that Barry had punched him. I heard him on the phone reporting this matter to the School Inspector, who had supported him at the P & C meeting.

During our drive home that afternoon, Ivan bragged, 'I'm way cleverer than that idiot, Barry. All my staff, including you, were witness to the fact that he hit me. That helps my stance regarding my refusal to allow his children to attend my school. What's even better is that he didn't touch me at all. He threatened to deck me, but he chickened out and left.'

It took me a moment to digest his words, 'But you have a graze on your chin.'

'Yeah. As I said, I'm way smarter than the average person. I picked up a stone from the garden and scraped my chin. It worked a treat because you and all my staff believed he hit me.'

'What? Why are you doing this to that innocent family? Are you demented? They were protecting their child, and now you are out to destroy them!'

'That's right. Anyone who questions me will pay a serious price, mark my words.'

As he stopped the car in our garage, I bounded into the house and into my bedroom. I slammed the door and locked it. I, too, was scared to be around this out-of-control NARCISSIST.

Waking to a Nightmare
Deceived by a Charming, Narcissist Paedophile

Ivan banged on the door, 'Open this door. I need to talk to you.'

I drew my face out of the pillow I was sobbing into and managed to say, 'Go away. I can't even look at you right now.'

Later that evening, when I left my room, Ivan grabbed my arms and dug his long fingers into them. 'Aminia, you will shut your mouth about this, or I will have to shut it for you.'

'Ivan, I don't understand why you are so hell-bent on hurting this family. You know they told the truth. Inka should be the one that had to leave the school.'

He pulled me roughly towards him and growled, 'I am the principal, and I have the right to refuse any child I decide is unfit to attend my school. And that, my darling wife, is the end of the matter. If you continue to argue with me about this, there will be dire circumstances for you. So shut your mouth and do your wifely job of supporting me.'

Waking to a Nightmare
Deceived by a Charming, Narcissist Paedophile

I pushed away from him, 'I can no longer live with you. You make me feel sick just looking at you!'

In an instant, his demeanour changed. He held me to his chest while gently stroking my back and whispered, 'Aminia, please! Think of what will happen…' He used his most potent weapon to manipulate me, my children. With a finger under my chin, he forced me to look into his eyes. 'Think about our children. Surely you realise how adversely they will be affected if I lose my job. You must realise that all my actions have been to protect them and us. Now let's have a wine and calm down, and soon things will settle.'

But things did not settle within me.

I could see clearly how he gaslighted me and controlled me with his erratic and confusing behaviour swings. As I write this, I feel a chill running up my spine; He is not a man. He is a monster born from the depths of hell, a poisonous spider, weaving his deceitful web tightly around me as he devoured my essence.

Waking to a Nightmare
Deceived by a Charming, Narcissist Paedophile

However, this time, a spark in me ignited a rebellious flame that would not be extinguished. I took the rest of the week off. And thank goodness Ivan left to attend a conference. Of course, Sharlet went with him. I frantically tossed around my options in my fevered mind. My parents became worried about me and decided to visit. When I told them what had happened, they begged me to leave with the children and go to live with them. I knew this would not be good for Kathy and Mitch because they were happy and settled in their schools, and we had moved them too often.

Something inside me snapped. It was time to respect myself and take control and responsibility for my well-being. Even though I knew it would be perhaps the most challenging thing I had ever done, I had to change my situation for myself and my children.

I ordered Ivan out of the house and threatened to report him to higher authorities if he did not leave. He left.

Waking to a Nightmare
Deceived by a Charming, Narcissist Paedophile

I slept on and off that night, tossing and turning in my bed. Finally, I fell into an exhausted sleep. My daughter's voice woke me...

'Dad, get off me! Leave me alone! I was asleep!'

I glanced at the clock—1:57 a.m. My feet hit the floor.

Standing at my daughter's bedroom door, my blood ran cold. It was as if the whole world had ceased to exist... and only this moment was left, gnawing at my insides.

My husband, Ivan, was lying on top of my 14-year-old daughter.

'Get off her', I screamed.

My precious daughter looked over her father's shoulder and begged, 'Go away, Mum. Just go.'

At that moment, I felt Mitch put his arm around my waist, and he led me away.

THIS CREEPY SPIDER WAS NOT ONLY A NARCISSIST. HE WAS A VENOMOUS PAEDOPHILE!

Waking to a Nightmare
Deceived by a Charming, Narcissist Paedophile

CHAPTER 16

Although Ivan had packed and left, things got worse with every passing second at the school. Ivan called me into his office and said, 'Aminia, you can keep working as the school's Office Manager and Casual Teacher. I'm taking Sharlet on a holiday, and Inka is staying with another parent.'

The next day, he returned and asked me not to tell anyone about his behaviour. My eyes glistened as fury burned within me, and I spat my words at him, 'You have no right to ask me that. I will say whatever I need to! I have already consulted a solicitor, and I'm beginning divorce proceedings.'

Ivan's NARCISSISTIC nature exploded to the surface. He sprang at me and held me by my throat over my desk. I gasped for air. For a split second, I lost all sense of what was happening. He let go when he heard someone coming into the office. I slumped on my chair, gasping for air.

Waking to a Nightmare
Deceived by a Charming, Narcissist Paedophile

I knew that he wouldn't let me be. So, on my way home, I rang my solicitor to report the incident. 'Are you alright? She gasped.

'No, not really. It is hard for me to speak. Ivan lost control when I said I would not do as he asked. He tried to strangle me.'

'That's dangerous and extreme behaviour. I will support you in implementing a restraining order against Ivan A.S.A.P.'

Two days after Ivan's leave began, one of the Inspectors who had attended the parents' and citizens' meeting visited me at the school and said, 'I have been concerned about aspects of the story your husband gave us regarding the incidents with the young boys and Inka. Would you care to tell me what you know about it?'

I stared at him, then my words fired at him, 'You dare to come to me now and ask me what happened. You and your cronies were all busy covering your backs. You vilified that family, and now those poor little innocent boys must leave home at 7.30 a.m. to catch the High School Bus and return late in the afternoon. How would you feel if they were your children? Do you have children? He nodded, 'Then wouldn't you have done the same as those boys' parents did to protect them? Inka should have left the school, not them. You all disgust me.'

The meek and mild me died that day. I knew I was dealing with a monster, a wolf in sheep's clothing. And worse still was the fact that those people who had the authority to put a stop to his behaviour chose instead to protect him and, therefore, enable him to continue his dangerous narcissistic behaviour, not only with me but with innocent children and their parents.

Not long before Ivan was due to return to school after his leave, a representative from the Department of Education informed me that they were moving me to another school about twenty kilometres away. The headmaster there was a

Waking to a Nightmare
Deceived by a Charming, Narcissist Paedophile

friend of Ivan's and sided with him. Ivan often phoned me during work hours to harass me about how he wanted the legal aspects of our separation to be sorted. I refused to talk to him about this while working and hung up on him. My new boss called me into his office and said, 'Aminia, you will treat Ivan with the respect he deserves. If you hang up on him again, I will deal with you severely.'

I was stunned and felt exhausted, but I somehow found my voice. 'Surely it is your role to protect your staff. It was Ivan who was at fault. He had no right to phone here about our private matters. Please ask him not to do that.' He dismissed me with a curt wave, and I knew not to expect any support from him.

That afternoon, Kathy saw I was upset. She sat beside me and said, 'Mum, you've got to understand. It's like this: there is a castle; Dad and I live inside the castle, and you and Mitch live outside it. And I am Daddy's girlfriend, not you…'

Waking to a Nightmare
Deceived by a Charming, Narcissist Paedophile

It felt like a large part of me died in that moment, and I couldn't think. I reached out and pulled her into my chest as my large tears plopped into her hair. How was I to respond to this? I knew that these weren't her words. They had been fed to my little girl by her narcissistic peodophile father! Kathy pulled away from me and shouted as she ran to her room. 'I'm leaving and going to live with my dad.'

I sank onto the floor. My entire body shook, and tears fell into my lap, soaking my clothes. This was when I knew my relationship with my daughter would never be the same. I was devastated.

THIS NARCISSIST'S TACTICS HAD NO BOUNDARIES.

Waking to a Nightmare
Deceived by a Charming, Narcissist Paedophile

CHAPTER 17

The restraining orders my solicitor helped me apply for were still pending. Ivan came to the farm to persuade me to drop them. I reported this to my solicitor. Within the hour, she informed me that she had contacted his solicitor and told him that Ivan was to keep his distance from me, or things could become more difficult for his client. Ivan's solicitor assured her he would pass this warning on to his client. That afternoon, Ivan's solicitor rang my solicitor and informed her Ivan had agreed not to go near me.

But, true to his form, Ivan believed he still could manipulate me to his will. He kept coming down to the house and being attentive and friendly to me in front of the children. He was pretending he was a changed man. On one occasion, I arrived home, and he had the makings of a full-baked dinner. I asked what he expected me to do with the food. 'Sharlet cannot cook like you do. She has no idea how to cook a decent

Waking to a Nightmare
Deceived by a Charming, Narcissist Paedophile

baked dinner. Can't you do that and let us be with the kids like old times.' The children were listening and begged me to let him stay. My children's pleading faces caused me to bend to their wishes. True to Ivan's style, he took that to mean I forgave him, until the next time he arrived with food, I declared, 'You cook your own baked dinner. I'm going out.'

'No, you are not! You will stay here and prepare our meal!' Aminia, please! Listen to me! I have a proposition for you. What if Sharlet and I lived in the top house, and you and the kids could continue to live here? I can take care of Sharlet and you.' (There were two houses on our 100-acre property, and I used the top one for my art studio.)

I pushed past him and picked up my handbag, ready to leave. Ivan stepped in my way. I hit him with my handbag and tried to get around him. He tripped me. I fell hard onto the floor. Kathy was in her room doing her homework. Her head snapped up when she heard my scream, followed by a thud.

Waking to a Nightmare
Deceived by a Charming, Narcissist Paedophile

Ivan pounced on me and wrapped his long fingers around my throat. My feet thrashed, but he only tightened his deadly grip. I could not breathe, and my mind rang with the chilling thought… 'I am going to die.'

Kathy screamed, 'Get off my mother! You are killing her!'

Ivan's shocked face swivelled towards his daughter. His mouth gaped, 'I, I didn't know you were home', he stuttered as he scrambled off me. I grabbed my handbag and tried to push past him to the door. All I wanted to do was to escape the clutches of this maniac. Ivan's reflexes were lightning-fast. He grabbed my arm and twisted it behind my back. Kathy screamed. He loosened his grip, and I bolted out the door. He chased me to the garage. As I slipped into my car, he grabbed the door and held it open. I screamed, 'Let me go!'

'No! If you drive off, you will take the door off on the way.'

Waking to a Nightmare
Deceived by a Charming, Narcissist Paedophile

'I don't care!' I planted my foot on the accelerator. He let go of the door…it swung shut, and I tore out of the garage, leaving a cloud of dust behind me.

A couple of days later, when he arrived, I was tending some cattle down in the bottom paddock. As he approached me, I warned him to stay away from me. He raised his hands in the surrender position and smiled. 'Come on, Aminia; there is no need for all of this. You know I love you, and I always will. Just give me six to twelve months to get her out of my system, and I'll come back to you. Please, have faith in me. You're the true love of my life; surely you know that. Things just got a little out of kilter lately. All the accusations against me have stressed me. Deep inside, you know how much I love you. To err is human. I slipped a few times and did things I would not normally do. I was a fool. Please, give me one last chance. I will always be there for you, and nothing like this will ever happen again!' He crossed his heart and opened his arms wide.

Waking to a Nightmare
Deceived by a Charming, Narcissist Paedophile

At that moment, something inside me exploded. He stepped towards me. I raised my arms and pushed him hard; he landed on his bum in front of me. A snarling voice I didn't recognise fired at him, 'Don't you dare touch me! I don't want you back. You make me want to vomit when I look at you! You are a disgusting monster!'

He rolled over, hauled himself up, and reached out to touch me again. I jumped away and shouted, 'Don't you dare lay a finger on me, you poor excuse for a man.' He reached for me again, and I pushed him hard on his chest. As he stumbled backward, I hurled a barricade of expletives at him. His knees buckled, and he sunk to the ground. His hands reached up to me as he gasped, 'Aminia! You don't swear!'

It was true; I had never used foul language before. I surprised myself that I even knew such words. But in that moment, those words gave me the strength to stand up to him, and it felt liberating. Elation filled me as I watched him scamper off. I felt powerful, 'Go on, run like a scared rabbit. You sicken me, you creep!' I shouted.

THE COMPLIANT VICTIM HAD FOUND HER VOICE; SHE WAS STRONG.

Waking to a Nightmare
Deceived by a Charming, Narcissist Paedophile

CHAPTER 18

My joy was short-lived. I shivered with fear and anger as I drove. On the outskirts of town, I rang my solicitor and explained as much as possible. She could hear the rasp in my voice and advised me to get it checked by a doctor as soon as possible. I knew my throat was internally bruised. It was much more painful than when he had choked me the first time.

While making the phone call to my solicitor, I saw Ivan drive by. I was relieved that he didn't notice me. I sat shaking in my car, and then I saw Mitch go by in his friend's car. My children needed me. I turned my car around and headed home.

I arrived home about ten minutes after Mitch. I could hear Kathy talking to him behind her closed door. I gently knocked. Kathy's quiet, wavering voice asked, 'Who is there?' I informed her it was me. 'Please, Mum, leave us

Waking to a Nightmare
Deceived by a Charming, Narcissist Paedophile

alone. Mitch and I will see you in the morning.' I walked away on shaking legs. I couldn't sleep. I sat in my lounge chair and kept a vigil eye on the farm road leading to our door.

Neither of the children emerged from Kathy's room until the next morning. Their faces still wore the streaks of their tears, and they would not look at me. I tried to calm them and begged them to get ready for school. Kathy spoke with her back turned to me, 'Mum, we are not going to school. We want to stay home.' She grabbed her brother's hand, dragged him into her room, and slammed the door.

A little later, my twelve-year-old son, Mitch, came out and said, 'Mum, how do you expect us to go to school today? We both feel sick, and we don't want to have to explain anything to our teachers.'

My heart ached for my children. I could not afford to miss a day's work. As I explained earlier, my new boss was not sympathetic to my situation. Before I left, I knocked on

Waking to a Nightmare
Deceived by a Charming, Narcissist Paedophile

Kathy's door. I was surprised when she opened it. I drew my children into my arms and instructed them to be vigilant and lock the door from the inside. 'If your father comes here, you must keep the door locked and quietly phone me. Do not let him know you are home. Do you understand?' They both nodded. As I drove away, I was almost choking on the lump in my throat, and I swiped my tears away.

At around 11:30 a.m., Kathy called me and whispered, 'Mum, please come. Dad is here, and we are scared.'

I grabbed my belongings, told the school principal I was not feeling well and left. On my way, I rang my solicitor and explained the situation. She pleaded, 'Aminia, do not go near Ivan. I will ring the police and inform them of the situation. Can someone meet you at your gate and wait until the police arrive?'

I rang my neighbour and explained the situation. He agreed to meet me. During my frantic drive home, my solicitor rang

Waking to a Nightmare
Deceived by a Charming, Narcissist Paedophile

and said the police were coming. When I arrived at the farm gate, the police and my neighbour were waiting for me.

As I led the way up my drive, I began to shake. *Were my children safe? I should have been home with them.*

Ivan was in the laundry doing his washing and wearing nothing but his underpants. Where he was living with Sharlet, in the bush as a 'hippy', there weren't any facilities for washing his clothes.

The senior officer explained to Ivan the reason they were there. I was shocked by the officer's comment: 'We know, mate. These women want to get you out of their hair so they can live without any contact with you. We see this a lot, and I bet you never laid a hand on her.'

'No, I would never do that.' Ivan responded.

Neither the police nor Ivan knew the children were inside listening. Suddenly, Kathy shot out the door screaming, 'You liar, Dad, you tried to kill my Mum!'

Waking to a Nightmare
Deceived by a Charming, Narcissist Paedophile

I was standing on the lawn below the verandah when Ivan jumped off and grabbed me. The police officers were shocked and hesitated before jumping into action. They caught one of Ivan's arms each and frog-marched him to their car. The sergeant came back and apologised to me and asked if there was anywhere I could go to be safe. I informed him that I had a doctor's appointment set for me by my solicitor and needed to go into town.

'You wait here with your children while we speak with your husband.' When the sergeant returned, he said, 'I warned your husband he is not to come anywhere near you again because we will arrest him. Does he have any firearms?'

My shaky voice informed him that Ivan had a rifle.

Displaying a different demeanour towards me, the sergeant said, 'We are worried about your safety. He is out of control and is likely to be one of those people who could blow you away.'

Waking to a Nightmare
Deceived by a Charming, Narcissist Paedophile

Both the children heard this conversation and were visibly traumatised. After the police officers followed Ivan off the property, I tried to convince Kathy and Mitch to go with me to the doctor, but Kathy refused, and Mitch wanted to stay with his sister.

I could not miss my appointment with the doctor, so I left after telling the children to keep the door locked and not to open it to anyone, especially their father. Luckily, I had thrown away Ivan's set of keys that he had left behind. They landed high in the branches of an old tree.

As I drove out of the farm gate, I saw that the police had pulled Ivan over to the side of the road. He had left to go into town but had turned around and headed back. They waved me on. Later, the sergeant rang and told me they had gone to Ivan's place but could not find a weapon on the premises. Ivan told them he didn't have it anymore. After that, Ivan stayed away from the farm and me.

Waking to a Nightmare
Deceived by a Charming, Narcissist Paedophile

THIS DANGEROUS NARCISSIST SPIDER COWERED

IN THE FACE OF AUTHORITY

Waking to a Nightmare
Deceived by a Charming, Narcissist Paedophile

CHAPTER 19

The situation, however, had left me emotionally vulnerable. I could see that my children were traumatised and mentally disturbed by what they had witnessed.

I asked Mitch whether his father still owned his gun, 'Yeah, he does. He promised me only a few days ago that he would take me hunting when everything settled.' Ivan must have had his gun stashed somewhere, and the police couldn't find it.

I was always nervous when Ivan took Mitch out with his gun because one day, I noticed him leaning his rifle against the wire of a fence as they climbed over. I had strong words with him about that. Another disturbing habit he had was to leave his gun propped against our dressing table with the box of bullets lying beside it. I told him that if he didn't find a safe place where the children couldn't access it, I would take it up into one of the paddocks, dig a hole, bury it, and he would

Waking to a Nightmare
Deceived by a Charming, Narcissist Paedophile

never find it. I was unafraid to confront him when my children's safety was at risk.

In my frazzled state, I had forgotten my friend, Maree, was due to arrive at the start of the Christmas School Holidays. Before this drama happened, Ivan and I had promised our children we would take them on a holiday to Australia's top end. I decided my children, and I needed to get away. Maree agreed to go with us.

We packed. On the way, I stopped at the bank. I was delighted when I discovered Ivan had not withdrawn any cash from our holiday account. I withdrew it all and put it into my account. Although we did not go to the Top End, the holiday was a much-needed healing time for all of us.

Every time the scene of Ivan on top of Kathy in bed accosted my mind, I vomited. I also felt I was purging the horror of this scene and, more importantly, this despicable paedophile out of my system. Despite this, the holiday was exactly what

Waking to a Nightmare
Deceived by a Charming, Narcissist Paedophile

we all needed…fun and adventure. My children's laughter filled me with hope.

About an hour away from home, I had a hunch that Ivan and Sharlet were at the house. I phoned, and Ivan answered. 'What are you doing there? Is Sharlet with you?' He confirmed she was. I exploded, 'Get that woman out of my home right now! Neither of you should be there! How did you get in?'

He laughed, 'Aminia, you are so naive. There is more than one way to get into a house.'

As I walked inside, I was horrified. Broken glass was spread on the floor where Ivan had broken the window to climb in. The walls were devoid of paintings, including all my artwork. Also missing was my much-loved painting, which Ivan had bought me as a wedding present. The linen cupboard doors were swinging open. Some articles had been discarded on the floor. On closer inspection, I knew this devious pair had taken all the best linen, including the items

Waking to a Nightmare
Deceived by a Charming, Narcissist Paedophile

my grandmother had lovingly crocheted for my wedding trousseau.

I collapsed onto the floor. Maree sat beside me and hugged me to her. I sobbed, 'How could a woman do this to another woman?' Maree declared.

Interspersed by my sobbing, I managed to say, 'Because Sharlet is a narcissist and a paedophile as well.'

Maree questioned, 'I know she is a narcissist, but how do you know she is a paedophile?

'When Sharlet and I were collecting wood one day, she told me to wake up to myself, and this is what she said. 'It's up to the father to show his daughter how to be with a man and to the mother to teach her son how to be with a woman as I have done for my son.'

Maree's eyes bulged with horror as she uttered, 'They are both evil.'

Waking to a Nightmare
Deceived by a Charming, Narcissist Paedophile

CHAPTER 20

It took seven weeks before we were called to the local courthouse to finalise the restraining order against Ivan, who had protested it. My parents accompanied me. The magistrate sat up high behind a desk, and when it was our turn for him to deal with my case, Ivan stood in front of the bench like a naughty boy in front of the headmaster, hands clasped in front of him. I was sure Ivan was attempting to look innocent, portraying himself as the victim. I was aware of my narcissist husband's manipulating tactics and could see through his façade.

The magistrate said, 'I'm sorry, I have to rule in favour of your wife even though I know these women all do this to get their menfolk out of their hair.' My father began to rise out of his seat, and my mother placed a restraining hand on his arm.

Waking to a Nightmare
Deceived by a Charming, Narcissist Paedophile

It was evident the judge hadn't read the police report. These men were supposed to be protecting victims. My heart sank, and I felt vulnerable. But then something ignited inside me. It was time I stood my ground. No longer would I be intimidated by these types of men.

After the restraining order was officially signed, Ivan got one of his mates to break into the farmhouse and take all the photos of the children. He stripped the artwork I had done over several years from my studio. And even my files containing my essential documents.

I lay on the floor, feeling as though I had been violated. My body convulsed as my grief poured from me. Not even the law was keeping him restrained. He was doing whatever he could to hurt me.

To this day, I still lament the loss of my photos. I was the photographer for the family and would always ensure that all the beautiful moments were captured. He took away those precious memories. Now, I only have a handful of the photos

Waking to a Nightmare
Deceived by a Charming, Narcissist Paedophile

my mother took that captured the years before this narcissist's true nature rose with a vengeance against me.

Mum and Dad came to stay with me for a while. My father and helpful neighbour gathered firewood off the farm and stacked it in the shed. I spent my pent-up emotion chopping the wood to fit in my fireplace. While I was at work and Mum and Dad had gone shopping, Ivan again ignored his restraining order and came onto the farm. He loaded the trailer with all the firewood I had chopped and took it away. It was another attempt by Ivan to intimidate me.

When my father arrived home, he was furious and threatened to demand that Ivan return it. I burst into laughter. Dad's mouth dropped open, and his eyes popped. I'm sure he thought I'd lost the plot, 'Aminia, why are you laughing?'

Taking a big breath to settle my crazy, wonderful sense of humour, I blurted between more spurts of laughter, 'Don't bother Dad. As I chopped that wood, I let all my anger out on those pour blocks of wood, and now he and Sharlet will

Waking to a Nightmare
Deceived by a Charming, Narcissist Paedophile

be surrounded by that anger as they burn the wood!' Dad hugged me to him, and we danced around the shed.

In the meantime, more revelations about Ivan started coming to light. Ivan bragged to all the women with whom he had affairs that he would soon inherit a large amount of money from his wealthy childless relatives. In one of my exchanges with Sharlet, she admitted she went after him because she was tired of living the hippy life with her then-partner and wanted the good life Ivan offered her.

Waking to a Nightmare
Deceived by a Charming, Narcissist Paedophile

CHAPTER 21

Shortly after this, Kathy was admitted to hospital, supposedly suffering an appendix attack. The doctors were perplexed because they couldn't feel anything wrong with her appendix. They ran all the tests but found nothing wrong.

While I sat beside my daughter in the hospital, she said, 'Mum, I could die. Ring Dad and tell him to come and visit me.' I had no choice; I couldn't see her in pain and misery like this. I phoned her father. His phone rang out, so I left a message. Ivan did not come.

I called his mother to ask if she knew where Ivan was. Her venom accosted me, 'You bitch, you have devastated my son's life with your jealousy.'

My ire rose, and I replied, 'You mean I am responsible for your narcissist peodophile son's behaviour? That is rich coming from you. You told me you didn't even love him. So,

Waking to a Nightmare
Deceived by a Charming, Narcissist Paedophile

I think your attitude towards him may have contributed to his character.' I slammed the phone down.

Eventually, Kathy did have an operation, and the doctors said the appendix was healthy.

Time marched on, and Kathy had not seen her father for several weeks. Ivan rang Kathy and asked her to meet with him. Of course, I was reluctant to let her do that. It was dangerous. Finally, I gave in to Kathy's persistent nagging and agreed. I insisted they meet in a public place, a café in town. I parked across the road and a little up where I could see them sitting near the window. When they came out of the café, I picked Kathy up.

Kathy sat brooding and didn't say anything as I drove home. Later, I was weeding the garden. Kathy came and sat on the verandah. I sat beside her, and without warning, she turned on me, 'If you ever say anything about Dad and me, I will call you the liar.' I was speechless. Kathy jumped up, raced across the paddock, mounted her horse and rode it bareback up into the bush. This pulled the ground from under my feet. I was shivering with fear, petrified about my daughter's safety. My tears filled many tissues before I heard her thump into her room as night was falling.

True to Kathy's word, she has since called me a liar. She has always blamed me for her father's behaviour. Her father had been playing with my poor child's mind for most of her life. Even as I write this, I feel deep sadness and a deep sense of helplessness.

How did he turn Kathy's mind so she believed he was the wounded person? Ah yes! I recalled his fateful words, *'You can make a child believe anything. All you have to do is say it the right way and often.'*

Since then, I have read articles about narcissists, and I am now aware of how difficult it is for an abused victim to get away from their abuser. He wove his thick web around his daughter, and to this day, he still influences her thinking.

Waking to a Nightmare
Deceived by a Charming, Narcissist Paedophile

One day, I was shopping in town when the school bus driver's wife asked me to have coffee with her. After we sat down, she informed me that her husband had told her that Kathy had a fight with Inka on the bus. 'My husband was horrified when Inka screamed these words, *'Your father had sex with me, and he loves me, not you.'* Punches were thrown, so my husband stopped the bus and told the girls to get off because they were disturbing the other children. He said they were fighting like a pair of cats.' (At that time, Inka lived with Ivan and Sharlet). I was horrified.

This highlighted Kathy's mental state. She was volatile and was acting in a manner that showed her mental unrest. I came across a quote by Laura Davis where she talks about a child who has gone through such manipulation, *"Abuse manipulates and twists a child's natural sense of trust and love. Her innocent feelings are belittled or mocked, and she learns to ignore her feelings."*

Waking to a Nightmare
Deceived by a Charming, Narcissist Paedophile

THIS MASTER MANIPULATOR HELD COMPLETE CONTROL OVER MY DAUGHTER.

CHAPTER 22

Not long after our divorce was complete, I moved to another town; I wanted a new beginning. I finally got a job in another school. One day, an Indigenous Dancing Group visited the school, and I was appointed to look after them. I asked where they came from. One said, 'Hey Miss, ain't you the misses of that fella who was the headmaster at that school?' I nodded. 'Yeah, he's the one that had that affair with that troublemaker, Jan. She had his baby.'

I asked, 'How do you know the baby was Ivan's?'

They all snickered, and the talkative one said, 'Ah, Miss, that boy is the spit out of that man's mouth. He's got the same reddish-blond hair and looks the same as him.'

I am sure a few of you might wonder why I didn't leave Ivan earlier. 'In my defence, I loved my life outside of Ivan's behaviour. I was afraid that I would lose contact with my daughter and Mitch would lose his sister. And that is precisely what happened.

Waking to a Nightmare
Deceived by a Charming, Narcissist Paedophile

PART 1—THE EPILOGUE

As I draw towards the end of this part of my story, I know I could have written about Ivan's many other affairs, but that would have filled too many pages. Suffice it to say that Ivan always chose the young women teachers or the mothers with young girls.

Ivan is a narcissistic paedophile who caused much harm and trauma to not only me but also to several others, as my story shows. Writing is the only way I can use my voice, which Ivan, the Narcissist, Peodophile, has shut down at each step. This is the only way to expose Ivan's character and highlight how a narcissist can cleverly manipulate those around them.

I paid a heavy price for Ivan's sins. Yet, here I am, having gone through trauma after trauma, writing my memoirs, which is a cathartic experience…THERE IS MORE …

PART 2...

THE NEXT

GENERATION

Waking to a Nightmare
Deceived by a Charming, Narcissist Paedophile

As I embark on the second part of my journey, I am aware that my mind is rarely free from the trauma of what happened to my daughter. I constantly worried about my granddaughters. They were reaching the same age Kathy was when I discovered what Ivan was doing to her. It was a nightmare, and I was living in it. The image of my husband in bed with Kathy haunted my mind constantly...

Waking to a Nightmare
Deceived by a Charming, Narcissist Paedophile

CHAPTER 1

In January, my mother turned 90, and I decided to throw a party to celebrate this milestone. I invited Mum's family members and her friends.

The party was a great success. The house buzzed with laughter. At the end of the evening, most guests either went home or stayed in motels in the area. My longtime friend, Sharon, whom I had met when I first moved out of Sydney, stayed overnight as she had travelled the furthest.

My granddaughter, Tanya, stayed with me while she worked at her uncle Mitch's café over the Christmas school break. Tanya was born on New Year's Day and was about to turn 15. I prepared breakfast while my mother, Sharon, and Tanya conversed at the table. I heard Mum ask Tanya, 'Are you still doing singing lessons with Sharlet?' Ivan and Sharlet had married not long after he and I split up.

Waking to a Nightmare
Deceived by a Charming, Narcissist Paedophile

Tanya replied, 'Yes, I love singing.' Then she paused, and when she spoke again, her words dripped with venom, 'But I hate having to stay overnight at Granddad's place. The sharp sound of my pan dropping in the sink shattered the poignant silence in the room. I darted into the seat next to my granddaughter.

My mother asked, 'Tanya, why? '

Tanya's eyes filled with tears and then leaked down her cheeks; her voice hitched as she blurted these chilling words, 'Every time I'm there, he comes into my room and does stuff to me.'

I was speechless; bile rose in my throat. I couldn't speak.

Sharon asked, 'Tanya, what does he do to you?'

Tanya fiddled with her spoon in her lap and lowered her eyes. Then she drew a breath and whispered through trembling lips, 'He climbs into bed and touches me,' I placed my hand over Tanya's and whispered, 'What do you mean

Waking to a Nightmare
Deceived by a Charming, Narcissist Paedophile

when you say, *'He touches me?'*. She stared into her lap and hunched her shoulders as she tried to hold back her tears. I remained quiet, giving her time to find her voice. After a few minutes, she raised her red eyes to me and, between sobs, uttered words that assaulted every fibre of me, 'He... He does sex stuff to me.'

Unbidden, my mind flew to an incident when Tanya was about three and a half years old. She was staying with me and my second husband, Keith. Tanya, who had been toilet trained, had begun wetting herself again.

While changing her nappy in the morning, I realised I had left her cream on the sideboard. Keith was walking by, and I asked him to hand it to me. Tanya became agitated and shrieked, 'No, Poppy, I don't want you to put the cream on me,' Keith never changed her nappy and was shocked at her reaction. He threw the cream over to me and bolted out the door.

Waking to a Nightmare
Deceived by a Charming, Narcissist Paedophile

A few days before this incident, Kathy told me she had bought and read a book to Tanya about *Good Touching and Bad Touching.* Kathy told me it was appropriate for children aged three to five.

I gathered Tanya into my arms and spoke soothing words into her ear until she became calm. As I changed her nappy, I questioned Tanya regarding who changed her at each place I knew where she would have been minded and needed her nappy changed. I left Ivan and Sharlet's names until last. When I mentioned Ivan, Tanya became agitated and, between hiccupped sobs, declared, 'Poppy Ivan does, and it hurts.' I asked her to show me where he hurt her, and she pointed between her legs.

When Keith returned, I told him what Tanya had said. He had two daughters, and his reaction was sheer horror. 'Aminia, you must tell Kathy about this.'

I spent many agonising hours trying to work out how to approach this subject with Kathy. This was a highly sensitive issue between us, and I needed to be careful about presenting this alarming subject to her.

THIS SPIDER'S VENOMOUS WAYS HAD TO BE STOPPED.

Waking to a Nightmare
Deceived by a Charming, Narcissist Paedophile

CHAPTER 2

The following day, Keith drove Tanya and me to Kathy's home, an hour's drive south. I sat in silence the whole way. Keith glanced at me often but did not speak. I'm sure he sensed I needed to have thinking time. He was right.

After finishing the morning tea Kathy served, she took the dishes to the kitchen and washed them. Keith hugged me and said, 'Don't fret; you will find the right words. He picked Tanya up and said, 'Come on, I will take you for a walk.'

I couldn't delay any longer. I drew a long, settling breath and entered Kathy's kitchen. 'Kathy, I have something important to tell you,' I repeated what Tanya had told me. 'Kathy, what concerns me is that Tanya informed me you read the book about *Good and Bad Touching* to her.'

Kathy's shoulders slumped, and she turned her pale face towards me. After a poignant moment's hesitation, her demeanour changed, and her face turned bright red. 'She is a liar. I have *not* read that book to Tanya.' I reminded her that she had recently told me she had read the book to Tanya. Kathy's face morphed into a picture of sheer horror. Then she sneered and spat her words into my face, 'She is a little liar, and you are stupid to believe her.'

'Kathy, calm down. Children Tanya's age do not make things like this up, and yes, I believe her!'

'Kathy screamed, 'Get out of my house and take that little brat with you! You are just making trouble for Dad!' To my horror and true to her form, my daughter protected her father.

A couple of months after this disturbing incident, another arose. Kathy, prone to running hot and cold towards me, invited Keith and me to attend the birthday party of her youngest daughter, Hanna. Keith was reluctant to go because he didn't want me to be hurt any further by my daughter's erratic behaviour. I reminded him she was my only daughter and the mother of my grandchildren. And so, we went. My

Waking to a Nightmare
Deceived by a Charming, Narcissist Paedophile

ex-husband also attended with Sharlet. Keith protected me and took me away from them.

When Kathy announced that lunch was served, Ivan and Tanya were missing. Mitch's daughter, Isabelle, who was eleven, offered to find them. Soon, she returned and was visibly shaken. She pulled me aside and told me she had seen Ivan with Tanya curled up in the corner of a tent pitched in the far corner of the large backyard. Kathy overheard her, and when I turned to go to the tent, she pushed me aside and snarled, 'I will go and get them. You stay here!' When she returned, her face was ashen. Just then, I noticed Ivan and Sharlet getting into their car. They sped off.

Kathy approached me and asked, 'Mum, please don't say anything. But I want you to take Tanya back to your place for a while.' Of course, I agreed. I was hoping that, finally, my daughter would realise how dangerous her father's obsession with Tanya was. She promised me that if she found out he was doing anything untoward with Tanya, she would personally report him to the police.

***

Now, I sat stunned by what the teenaged Tanya was saying…that she was still suffering sexual abuse at the hands of her grandfather, Ivan.

While my mind struggled to take this in, Sharon said, 'Tanya, what do you want to do about this?'

'I just want him to stop.'

Drawing a settling breath, I was finally able to speak. 'Have you spoken to your mother about what he does to you?' Tanya lowered her eyes and nodded. 'What did she say?' I asked in trepidation of what her answer would be.

Tears welled in Tanya's eyes. When she answered, she hesitated on every word. 'Mum was angry with me. She said I was being dramatic and was making things up.' Tanya

Waking to a Nightmare
Deceived by a Charming, Narcissist Paedophile

turned pleading eyes toward me, 'You believe me, don't you, Nan?'

All I managed was a nod. I felt sick. How could my daughter refuse to acknowledge her daughter's truth? I knew Tanya was not making this up. How could she accurately describe what I had witnessed her grandfather doing to her mother? I had never spoken to Tanya about this before now. I needed time to think.

THIS SPIDER HAD INJECTED HIS LETHAL VENOM INTO MY DAUGHTER. SHE WAS UNDER HIS SPELL.

After Sharon left, Mum, Tanya, and I visited Lenny, a longtime treasured friend who had invited us for morning tea. While Lenny, Mum, and I talked at his kitchen table, Tanya and a young lady friend of Lenny's daughter moved to another room. I could hear them talking, but not what they said.

Waking to a Nightmare
Deceived by a Charming, Narcissist Paedophile

During the drive home, I noticed Tanya was quiet. I glanced at her in the rearview mirror. Her head was resting on the window. She startled me when she said, 'Nan when we get home, could you help me look up the *Kid's Help Line* phone number?

I met her eyes in the mirror again, 'Why do you want the phone number of *Kid's Help Line*, Tanya?

'Because I want to report my grandfather for sexually molesting me'. Sheer determination was reflected in her eyes, and I felt trepidation.

COULD THIS BRAVE YOUNG GIRL UNRAVEL THIS SPIDER'S WEB.

Waking to a Nightmare
Deceived by a Charming, Narcissist Paedophile

CHAPTER 3

My mind was in a spin. I recalled how the police had treated me when I tried to report what Ivan had done to Kathy. But worse still, would Kathy turn on both of us?

After we arrived home, Tanya asked me for the phone book. I sat her down beside me and tried to persuade her not to rush into doing things.

Tanya took my hand and turned her determined face towards me. 'Nan, I've got to do this. What if he does the same to my sister? Someone must stop him, and I can do that. And besides, don't worry, Nan. Rachel (the young woman Tanya had spoken to at Lenny's) assured me I could speak to them confidentially, and I didn't have to give them my name if I didn't want to.'

Waking to a Nightmare
Deceived by a Charming, Narcissist Paedophile

What was I to do? Tanya was right; her grandfather had to stop his hideous actions. Her talking to someone outside the family could help her.

Tanya asked me to sit beside her while she made the call. I understood the kind of mental torture Tanya was suffering, and so I resolved to give her whatever support I could. During the call, the woman on the other end asked Tanya if she was with an adult. Tanya replied, 'Yes, my Nan is right beside me. The lady asked if she could speak to me.

Tanya passed the phone into my shaking hand. The female voice on the other end asked me to state my name and relationship to Tanya. Then her officious voice continued, 'Aminia, I'm sure you realise the serious nature of your granddaughter's issue and that it must be reported to the police.' In that instant, I felt sick. I did not… could not trust the police because of my past experiences.

The woman continued. 'Aminia, because it is the holiday period, we are short-staffed, and there is nobody I can call on who can help physically at this time. Can you assure me that Tanya can stay with you and be kept safe?' I affirmed my commitment to do so. She continued, 'And if anything changes, phone me immediately at this number?' She gave me the number, and I assured her I'd call if necessary.

The following morning, Tanya's father, Martin, rang and told her he would get her so she could spend time with her sister and brother. He wanted her to go with them to a concert in the town park where Ivan lived. Tanya's eyes pleaded with me. She put her hand over the receiver and whispered. 'What will I do?'

'Tell him you can't go with him because you're working at Mitch's shop for the rest of the week.'

Tanya relayed this message to her father, and I heard his explosive reaction. 'You are my daughter; you will do what I bloody tell you to do. I'm coming up to get you. And tell that fucking grandmother of yours to make sure you are ready to come home!'

Waking to a Nightmare
Deceived by a Charming, Narcissist Paedophile

Tanya's father worked for Ivan then, and I guessed Ivan had asked him to bring Tanya home. It is highly likely that Martin was protecting his job by not refusing a request from his boss.

I rang Mitch at his café and told him that Tanya had rung *Kid's Help Line* and reported his father, Ivan, for sexually molesting her and that I had been made responsible for keeping Tanya safe. Mitch was stressed because the shop was full of people, and he couldn't talk right then. He whispered into the phone, 'Mum, be careful. Martin was just here screaming abuse about you. I told him to leave. As he flew out the door, he shouted, I'll show that mother of yours who's the boss of my child. I'll bloody well deck that meddling bitch and drag my daughter away from her!'

My hands shook as I rang the lady at *Kid's Help Line* and told her the situation. She instructed me to leave the house, drive somewhere safe, and ring her back.

Waking to a Nightmare
Deceived by a Charming, Narcissist Paedophile

Giving frantic instructions, I gathered Tanya and Mum into the car, drove up the road, and parked in a back street while I rang the woman back. She advised me to take Tanya somewhere where she would feel safe. I was at a loss to know where to take her, but the lady suggested the police station, and Tanya nodded. 'Yes, Nan, I want to go to the police. He won't be game to take me from there.'

On the way to the police station, I pleaded with Tanya not to tell the police about her grandfather sexually molesting her until everyone had all their facts straight. My terrible experiences with the law when I tried to protect Kathy and myself were attacking my mind. Tanya reached over and patted my shoulder, 'Don't worry, Nan, I won't mention Grandad; I will tell the police I don't want to go with Dad because I'll lose my job.'

Tanya did not like nor respect her father. At times, he had not treated her right, even when she was a small child. Kathy left him when Tanya was about six months old and came to live with Keith and me. She told me Martin came home drunk and abused her because Tanya cried when he woke her. I was horrified when she said he was wasted and pissed all over Tanya's room, and that was the catalyst that drove her to leave him.

VICTIMS OF PEODOPHILES OFTEN HAVE LOW SELF-ESTEEM.

Waking to a Nightmare
Deceived by a Charming, Narcissist Paedophile

CHAPTER 4

As we entered the police station, Tanya bolted to the counter where a policeman was standing and exclaimed, 'I want to report my grandfather for sexually assaulting me.' The officer told us to sit in the waiting room while he consulted with the lady police officer who handled these cases.

While we waited, Martin rang Tanya. She told him to leave her alone and that she was at the police station and was not going anywhere with him. Everyone there could hear him abusing her. She ended the call. Then she phoned her mother and told her she was never coming home to her and that she would live with me from now on.

The lady police officer introduced herself, 'Hello, my name is Verity. Come with me and tell me about your problem. I will do all I can to support you.' Tanya asked whether I could go in with her, and Verity affirmed that I could.

Waking to a Nightmare
Deceived by a Charming, Narcissist Paedophile

Martin had burst through the door a moment earlier and overheard this conversation. He pushed me aside and grabbed Tanya's arm. 'I'm her father, and that bitch has no rights! I will go in with her!'

Tanya screamed hysterically. 'I want my Nan with me. Leave me alone, Dad!' The two officers behind the counter intervened. One positioned himself between Martin and Tanya, and the other protected me.

Tanya kept repeating, 'I want my Nan to go in with me, not him!'

One of the police officers asked Tanya how old she was, and between her sobs, she managed to say, 'I just turned 15.' The officer declared she was of the age to decide for herself. And so, I would accompany her.

During the interview, Tanya told the whole story, leaving nothing unsaid. I remained quiet for the entire duration,

Waking to a Nightmare
Deceived by a Charming, Narcissist Paedophile

except for uttering one sentence when Tanya referred to her mother, Kathy. 'She is a victim too.'

The police officer took numerous notes during the gruelling interview, which took over an hour. Toward the end of the interview, another officer tapped on the door and informed Verity that Tanya's mother and her partner had arrived and were being detained, along with Tanya's father, in another part of the station.

Drawing a long inward breath, Verity, Tanya's interviewing officer, declared, 'Tanya, I'm sorry this took so long, but I had to record your entire report. The good thing is that I have enough to ensure you can get a restraining order against your grandfather, Ivan. Now I will leave you to relax while I talk to your mother and the others.

After about thirty minutes, Verity returned; her smile gave us hope. 'Tanya, your mother and father initially insisted that what your grandfather did was just his way of showing love for you and that you were overreacting. It took some time to finally convince them it was inappropriate behaviour towards a young teenager.' She placed a hand on Tanya's knee and said, 'When I return from my lunch break, Tanya, on your behalf, I will apply for a restraining order against Ivan. Now I suggest you go to lunch with Aminia and your great-grandmother, who has been patiently waiting for you.'

I could not believe what I heard and strongly protested, 'Verity, please, we must finalise this now! They will take her and work on her mind. I know them.'

Verity assured me that she had their word that they would support Tanya in staying with me and doing all they could to keep her safe.

'Aminia, again, I urge you to take Tanya to lunch. She must be hungry and exhausted by now.'

I continued to protest but to no avail.

As Tanya, Mum, and I left the police station, Kathy grabbed Tanya and tried to haul her towards her partner's van parked

Waking to a Nightmare
Deceived by a Charming, Narcissist Paedophile

across the road. Tanya's screams alerted two police officers, who ran out to see what was happening. Tanya stretched her arms towards me and screamed through her sobs, 'I want to go with my Nan!'

One of the officers asked me, 'What is your relationship to this young lady.'

He then asked Kathy what relation she was to Tanya, and she said, 'I am her mother.'

The officer declared, 'Well, the mother has the right to decide. I tried to explain the situation to him, but both police officers shrugged and walked away.

I stood in abject horror as I watched my daughter drag my granddaughter' to her partner's van. Tanya's screams sent shivers down my spine.

Mum drove us home as I could not see the road through the flow of my hot tears. Mum tried to soothe me, but I couldn't comprehend her words.

Waking to a Nightmare
Deceived by a Charming, Narcissist Paedophile

That night, I could not sleep. As I tossed and turned, I asked, 'Who is there to protect the innocent children if those representing the law do not do their job correctly.'

The next day, I considered reporting the negligence of the police persons concerned, but I had little faith that anything would come of it. I knew Tanya and I should have been kept safe in the Police Station until everything was finalised. The two officers who came to see about the commotion outside the station should have asked Tanya her age. The negligence that day put my granddaughter back into the hands of a paedophile.

I'M SURE THIS NARCISSIST PEODOPHILE WAS CONVINCED HE WAS INVINCIBLE NOW.

Waking to a Nightmare
Deceived by a Charming, Narcissist Paedophile

FOOTNOTES

The Narcissist part of my husband has acted true to form. He has managed to turn my daughter and her children against me. As stated in this memoir, my daughter Kathy had kept her word and sided with her father to convince all concerned that I was the deluded liar.

The only one I have had some contact with since is my daughter's second girl, Hannah. She was visiting Mitch, and he invited me to his house. Mitch was always trying to mend the bridges, and he was acutely aware of my sorrow for not having contact with my grandchildren.

At first, Hannah was standoffish, but after everyone else had gone to bed, she sat with me, and we talked until the wee hours of the morning. She told me how much she missed me and our talks.

Waking to a Nightmare
Deceived by a Charming, Narcissist Paedophile

Not long after Hannah got home, she was no doubt trapped again in the Narcissist's web. Ivan and his accomplice, Kathy, must have influenced her because I didn't hear from Hannah again until several years later when she contacted me via Facebook. She greeted me with, 'Hi Nan, how are you doing?'

I was delighted and replied, 'Hi, Hon, it is so good to hear from you. I've missed you so much.'

Her response was full of expletives, and she accused me of ruining her family. I answered her by saying, 'What I did to try and protect you and Tanya, I would do again. Her following message was even more explosive, and I ghosted her. I can only assume that the master Narcissist has influenced Hannah, too. I fear that he may also have abused her sexually.

The Narcissist/Paedophile has tried hard to turn my son against me. But Mitch knows the truth and always lands on the right of it.

Waking to a Nightmare
Deceived by a Charming, Narcissist Paedophile

BRAVEHEARTS

In 2014, I attended a speech by Hetty Johnston. I cried through that entire speech. Hetty was telling my story about her daughter's sexual abuse and the organisation she established to bring awareness to this issue.

After giving her closing comments, Hetty came down among the people, and I made a beeline for her. I thanked her for her speech and asked how I could become involved in spreading the word about the organisation she founded in 1997. Hetty informed me that anyone could start a chapter of Bravehearts. I returned home determined to educate people in my community about the project.

I called a public meeting and announced that I was forming a Bravehearts Chapter in my area. My heart swelled when several people agreed to become members.

At our inaugural meeting, we decided to conduct a Bravehearts Fun Day at the local RSL (Returned & Services

Waking to a Nightmare
Deceived by a Charming, Narcissist Paedophile

League of Australia) Club. The manager gave us outstanding support by offering a part of his venue and the outside lawned area for us to hold a fun day to launch our Chapter of Bravehearts. Many people stepped forward and freely offered their help. Food Vendors, Clowns, Bands, and rides for the children, including a Ferris wheel and pony rides.

Some of our committee members and I decorated the hall and the outside areas the night before the event. I had hurt my ankle and hobbled around on crutches, but this did not hinder me on the day. I think my delight in what we had achieved fired my adrenalin and helped mask any physical pain I suffered.

I cannot recall how much money we raised that day selling raffle tickets and from donations freely given. The treasurer took care of that aspect. I know it allowed me to get more brochures and signs done. I designed them and printed them off on my trusty printer.

Waking to a Nightmare
Deceived by a Charming, Narcissist Paedophile

Before long, people declared their desire to participate in my area's Bravehearts Committee, and I again put my trusty printer to work. I produced appropriate brochures to hand out when I spoke at schools, preschools, community groups, church groups, and any other place where I could get the word out.

A local Men's Group in our area helped me at various Market Day venues. I was present at every one of them, determined to let people know there was an organisation to support victims and their families. Sometimes, at these venues, I was accosted, primarily by men who accused me of being a troublemaker. But even more surprising, by a few women who had suffered abuse. The subject caused them painful memories.

Initially, I held the meetings in my home, but as the group grew, I approached the RSL club's manager about holding our meetings in his club. He graciously made one of the conference rooms available to us.

Waking to a Nightmare
Deceived by a Charming, Narcissist Paedophile

After four years, I was exhausted but pleased that I had achieved my goal. I decided to resign as President. No one wanted to take on the job, and I couldn't blame them. It was a gruelling task.

I attended another Bravehearts meeting until it was time for me to move on.

Bravehearts is an Australian child protection organisation dedicated to the prevention and treatment of child sexual abuse. Founded by Hetty Johnston AM, it has been working tirelessly to create a safer environment for children.

bravehearts.org.au

9 Byth St, Arundel Queensland 4214

(07) 5552 3000

Waking to a Nightmare
Deceived by a Charming, Narcissist Paedophile

20 YEARS ON, AND MY HEART ACHES WHEN I THINK OF THESE INNOCENT CHILDREN BEING INFLUENCED BY THIS DANGEROUS NARCISSIST PEODOPHILE. TANYA IS NOW A MOTHER. SHE MARRIED A MAN MUCH OLDER THAN HER AND SOON FELL PREGNANT…SHADES OF HER MOTHER. I'M NOT SURE WHETHER IT IS A BLESSING THAT SHE GAVE BIRTH TO A SON AND NOT A GIRL. SHE MOVED FAR AWAY FROM IVAN…WAS SHE PROTECTING HER SON? I'M SAD TO SAY I HAVE ONLY SEEN MY GREAT-GRANDSON ON SOCIAL MEDIA.

UNFORTUNATELY, MITCH HAS ALSO BEEN HURT BY THIS. HE CANNOT CONDONE HIS SISTER'S OR HIS NIECE'S ATTITUDE TOWARDS ME AND SAYS, 'MUM, KATHY AND HER DAUGHTERS HAVE HURT YOU TOO MUCH. IT IS BEST TO MOVE ON AND FORGET THEM.' FOR A LOVING GRANDMOTHER,

Waking to a Nightmare
Deceived by a Charming, Narcissist Paedophile

THIS IS A DIFFICULT ASK. I LIVE IN THE HOPE THAT ONE DAY, THEY WILL REMEMBER THAT I WAS THE ONE WHO TRIED TO PROTECT THEM.

MITCH INFORMED ME THAT KATHY'S YOUNGEST CHILD, A BOY, HAS MATURED TO BE A DECENT ADULT. KATHY GAVE HIM TO HIS FATHER TO RAISE. SADLY, I DO NOT SEE HIM EITHER.

NOW, TANYA LIVES IN TASMANIA, AND MITCH SAYS SHE IS AS TWISTED IN HER THINKING AS HER MOTHER. I HEARD THAT HANNAH REPORTED SHE WAS SEXUALLY ASSAULTED BY HER BOYFRIEND; I DO NOT KNOW IF SHE WAS SEXUALLY ASSAULTED BY HER GRANDFATHER, IVAN.

I STILL LIVE IN THE HOPE THAT THESE YOUNG ADULTS WILL ONE DAY MATURE ENOUGH TO FACE THE TRUTH AND REALISE…

I WAS NOT THE PROBLEM.

Waking to a Nightmare
Deceived by a Charming, Narcissist Paedophile

THE AUTHOR'S NOTE: I have often been asked whether writing this part of my memoirs brings up the pain. Yes, it does. But overriding that is the release I feel to have a voice, which is a cathartic experience.

I hope that others who have suffered similar experiences will find their voice.

The law moves very slowly regarding sexual assault, but of late, it seems to have listened to the brave women who have stepped forward and told their stories. I admire their courage.

Aminia Mayo is my pen name. I was advised not to use my own.

Stay brave, stay safe.

NOTE: In this account of parts of my life, all places, names, and references to dates or times have been changed to protect the innocent.

www.ingramcontent.com/pod-product-compliance
Lightning Source LLC
Chambersburg PA
CBHW051429290426
44109CB00016B/1487